Reaching for the
Invisible God

STUDY GUIDE

Resources by Philip Yancey

The Jesus I Never Knew
The Jesus I Never Knew audio
The Jesus I Never Knew Zondervan*Groupware*™
The Jesus I Never Knew Study Guide (with Brenda Quinn)
What's So Amazing About Grace?
What's So Amazing About Grace? audio
What's So Amazing About Grace? Zondervan*Groupware*™
What's So Amazing About Grace? Study Guide (with Brenda Quinn)
The Bible Jesus Read
The Bible Jesus Read audio
Reaching for the Invisible God
Reaching for the Invisible God audio
Reaching for the Invisible God Study Guide (with Brenda Quinn)
Where Is God When It Hurts?
Disappointment with God
The Student Bible (with Tim Stafford)
Church: Why Bother?
*Meet the Bible (*with Brenda Quinn)
Finding God in Unexpected Places
I Was Just Wondering
Soul Survivor

Books by Philip Yancey and Dr. Paul Brand

Fearfully and Wonderfully Made
In His Image
The Gift of Pain

Reaching for the Invisible God

STUDY GUIDE

Philip Yancey
WITH BRENDA QUINN

ZONDERVAN™

GRAND RAPIDS, MICHIGAN 49530

CONTENTS

The Christian life should come with a warning label: "Do Not Attempt This Alone!" Jesus came to found a church, and the fruit of his life grows best in groups of Christians struggling and growing together, rather than in isolation. In the book *Reaching for the Invisible God,* I get honest about the unexpected surprises that await the Christian: doubts, dry times, testings. I speak of the need to find "trustworthy doubt companions" to see you through some of those desert periods. I hope and pray that your study group becomes a safe place for you to open up and become vulnerable.

One of the beauties of a small group is its constant reminder that we are all progressing through different stages. Right now some people feel a close sense of the presence of God, are growing spiritually, and experience joy and peace. Others are questioning the basics of the faith, fighting depression, trying to reconcile bright promises with tragic reality. This is a completely normal pattern: the apostle Paul's letters show that even in the first century, different churches were experiencing different stages of growth. A small group reminds me that what I am going through now, I will not always be going through. It prepares me for curves in the path that lie ahead.

I have made myself vulnerable in this book, and I hope you follow the lead. Commit yourself, as a group, to reward honesty rather than punish it. Commit yourself to listen with compassion and concern, not to jump on other group members by offering quick and easy answers. Commit yourself to encourage and support those who are going through hard times, to weep with those who weep, even as you rejoice with those who rejoice. If you do that, you will likely find that my book simply offers a jumping-off place. The truly meaningful times will come out of your own sharing.

You can of course use this study guide for individual study as well. If you do, you should find that the questions build a bridge between my pilgrimage with God and your own. You may want to buy a blank notebook or personal journal (many bookstores sell these) in which to record your responses. Use this guide not as a textbook, feeling obligated to consider every question and fill in every blank, but rather as a series of suggestions. Linger over questions and exercises that arouse something inside you. Skip those that don't seem to speak to the heart, and adjust as necessary those activities included that are designed for a group. You may find that adding just one person to your study—a spouse or a close friend, perhaps—makes it much more meaningful.

Most of you, however, will be using this study guide within a group. I like that notion. Like coals in a fireplace, we gain heat from one another. I pray that no matter how you use this guide, it will encourage a lifelong process of walking with spiritual companions, not alone.

ADVICE FOR SMALL GROUPS

Brenda Quinn and I have worked together to adapt the content of *Reaching for the Invisible God* to a group setting. Ideally, a small group should not exceed twelve or at most fifteen members. Anything larger than that and you'll likely find yourself reverting to a teacher-student structure in which the group leader dominates the discussion. In each session, as you'll see, we encourage you to break into even smaller groups of four to six. Sometimes the best sharing takes place in these smaller groups, which some people find less intimidating.

We recommend choosing a leader in advance of each week's meeting (it need not be the same leader every week). This study guide recommends personal reflection and prayer in each session, and each session includes far more content than most groups can cover in a single meeting. A good leader can scout these questions and exercises in advance, deciding which seem most pertinent to the needs of your group. The more willing the leader is to open up and share from his or her life, the more willing the group will be, so if you are the leader, take the role seriously. Think and pray about the group throughout the week before each meeting.

We also strongly recommend that if you are using this study in a larger group, you choose individuals ahead of time to facilitate the smaller group discussion time. This discussion time will make or break your study experience, and we have found that if each small group contains a person who is prepared to keep discussion going, share openly, and draw out responses from quieter members, the small group experience is much more positive. Talk with these individuals about the importance of their role and encourage them to come prepared, having read the chapters and reviewed the questions.

The study guide works best of course if everyone in the group has read the book we're studying, *Reaching for the Invisible God*. We follow its content chapter by chapter. Yet we also realize that in a busy world some people, no matter how well intentioned, do not get around to reading material in advance. Others read it so far in advance that by the time the meeting rolls around, they can barely remember the content. For this reason we begin each session with a condensed summary of the chapters to be discussed. Some groups may choose to read this summary aloud to set the tone for the discussion to follow.

USING PERSONAL REFLECTION TO ENLIGHTEN OUR PILGRIMAGE

As I said in the preface to the book, I have, in a sense, been writing this book since the first day I felt a hunger to know God. My journey is unique because of the things that make me and my life unique: my personality, my background, my religious upbringing, my life circumstances, and more. Your journey will likely hold similarities to mine in some ways while also remaining unique because of who you are. Therefore in each session we have included a section in which you are encouraged to examine more deeply a particular part of yourself or your life that impacts your relationship with God. The section is titled "Grasping for Understanding of Myself, My God." This exercise is an integral part of each week's study, and whether you decide to include some of this exercise in class time or ask participants to set aside personal time for the reflection, we encourage you to utilize these exercises as fully as possible.

LEADING GROUP DISCUSSION

Although group study is highly valuable, it carries challenges. You'll find that group study mirrors the challenges experienced in the church, on a smaller and sometimes more intense scale. But don't let these challenges keep you from the bonding and growth achieved through life together. Enter with realistic expectations, knowing that as in all relationships, there will be irritations, times when you don't feel like being together, people you don't particularly like, and probably even a period of disillusionment with the group. This is normal, just as it is normal in every family and in every friendship. Press on together. Most often you will find that God will bless individuals and group relationships in deep and lasting ways that far outweigh the difficult times you encounter.

As you meet together, keep the discussion moving. Don't be afraid of short silences, especially at first when members are moving deeper into a topic. But don't let it die, either. During a pause you may ask, "Does anyone have thoughts on this issue?" If silence continues or discussion remains minimal, don't be afraid to admit it: "Why don't we feel like talking about this today?"

The discussion may be less than provocative in other ways. It may start to snowball, with everyone agreeing with each other. In such cases you may need to play "devil's advocate" and argue the other side of the issue to force people to really think. At other times a few vocal people may dominate the discussion. You can counteract this by calling on others who have something to say, by watching especially for timid group members who are afraid to jump in, and even by taking the talkative one(s) aside after the meeting and asking them to share the time a little better.

Here are some suggestions for communicating throughout the discussion.

- When you feel that the speaker is making assumptions: "Why do you believe that? What have you experienced that makes you think so?"
- When you feel yourself becoming angry or uncomfortable: "Is anyone else feeling uneasy about this?" Don't feel a need for all to come to agreement, but don't feel either that you should remain silent when you disagree with a statement. Further discussion will air feelings and prevent hidden emotions from erupting later in more destructive ways.
- When the main focus has been lost or an interesting point has been dropped amid further discussion: "Let's go back to the original question." "Could we go back to what was said earlier about _____?" "Could we talk a little more about _____?"
- When you sense the need to clarify: "Do you mean that the Holy Spirit never bestows the more charismatic gifts or simply that these are less common now than they were in the early church?"

- When you feel there is more to what someone is saying: "Do you know why you have felt this way?" "When did you first begin to feel this way?"
- When someone is obviously passionate about a viewpoint: Affirm their right to feel strongly and that they've been understood by summarizing their statement before agreeing or disagreeing: "You really feel strongly about this. You're saying that . . . ."
- When someone is sharing something difficult and personal: "I've felt that way, too. I can understand." "I haven't experienced that, so I appreciate your helping me to understand better what it was like."

Lastly (this probably goes without saying), be sensitive and respectful. Realize that many issues discussed in this study will be difficult, even controversial. They may challenge long-held assumptions and practices. Remember that it takes time to process new ideas—especially those related to the Bible, our way of life, and our relationship with God. Much thought will continue after a group discussion, so don't feel a need to find all the answers in an hour or two. Most of us will continue thinking about these issues for the rest of our lives.

A FINAL WORD

We encourage you not to feel hemmed in by the structure we set out in this study guide. Although the book contains twenty-three chapters, we have divided the content into twelve sessions for this study guide, combining two chapters in each session except the last. Each session provides guidelines as to how much time to spend in each section, assuming that you will be spending an hour meeting together. If you meet for longer than an hour, you will find it easy to adjust your time frame accordingly.

Keep in mind that some sessions contain more than enough content to cover two sessions. Review the whole study ahead of time to determine where you might want to stretch a session to two weeks. And if your group gets excited about the content of one session, by all means don't squelch the interest and slavishly turn to a new topic the next week. Follow up on the discussion.

The same principle applies to individual questions. Don't cut off a stimulating discussion out of some obligation to plow through every single question. Likewise, if your group bogs down, move on until you find something that seems to generate interest. Remember, this small group study is not a school assignment with a goal of finishing all the material. You can certainly return to unfinished questions at home to work through on your own, but don't feel an obligation to complete everything. Our goal is for you to encounter God—even as you look honestly at some of the difficulties inherent in doing so—and that may happen in unpredictable, unplanned ways. Allow room for God's Spirit to work in your group.

And by all means, have fun! You will grapple with some honest, and honestly difficult, challenges of the spiritual life. Yet our prayer is that as you look honestly at God, yourself, and others, you will also gain new-found hope in our God, invisible yet ever present.

THIRST — A LONGING FOR GOD

—⌇—

The excerpt below is from *Reaching for the Invisible God*.

How do you sustain a relationship with God, a being so different from any other, imperceptible by the five senses? I hear from an inordinate number of people struggling with questions like this—their letters prompted, I suppose, by books I've written with titles like *Where Is God When It Hurts?* and *Disappointment with God*.

I have lived most of my life in the evangelical Protestant tradition, which emphasizes personal relationship, and I finally decided to write this book because I want to identify for myself how a relationship with God truly works, not how it is supposed to work.

In carving my path I am following a map laid out by many others, the "great cloud of witnesses" who have preceded me. My struggles with faith have at least this in their favor: they come from a long, distinguished line. I find kindred expressions of doubt and confusion in the Bible itself. Sigmund Freud accused the church of teaching only questions that it can answer. Some churches may do that, but God surely does not. In books like Job, Ecclesiastes, and Habakkuk, the Bible poses blunt questions that have no answers. Very key.

—⌇—

As I began this book, I went to friends whom I respect as Christians. I asked this question: "If a seeking person came to you and asked how your life as a Christian differs from hers as a moral non-Christian, what would you tell her?"

Hebrews 12 (handwritten in left margin)

Perhaps the most poignant response came from a friend whose name is well known in Christian circles. He thought for some time before responding, and then said this:

> I have no trouble believing God is good. My question is more, What good is he? I heard awhile back that Billy Graham's daughter was undergoing marriage problems, so the Grahams and the in-laws all flew to Europe to meet with them and pray for the couple. They ended up getting divorced anyway. If Billy Graham's prayers don't get answered, what's the use of my praying? I look at my life—the health problems, my own daughter's struggles, my marriage. I cry out to God for help, and it's hard to know just how he answers. Really, what can we count on God for?

That final question struck me like a bullet and has stayed lodged inside me. I know theologians who would snort at such a phrase as one more mark of self-centered faith. Yet I believe it lies at the heart of much disillusionment with God. In all our personal relationships—with parents, children, store clerks, gas station attendants, pastors, neighbors—we have some idea what to expect. What about God? What can we count on from a personal relationship with him?

Chapter 2

———— ❧ ————

Christians claim there are times, though perhaps less frequent than we would lead others to believe, when we do make personal contact with the Creator of the universe. "I have seen things that make all my writings seem like straw," wrote Thomas Aquinas about one such encounter.

I too have felt the tug at times, a tug strong enough to jerk me out of cynicism and rebellion, strong enough to wrench my life in a new direction. Yet for long stretches, achingly long stretches, I have also sat with my headphones on (as did Jodie Foster in the movie *Contact*), desperate for some message from the other world, yearning for reassuring contact, and heard only static.

How can something as fundamental as a God who created us to know and love him become so tenuous? If God, as Paul told a sophisticated crowd of skeptics in Athens, "did this," meaning all creation, in order that we might reach out and find him, why not make himself more obvious?

Writers of the Bible lived in the "Holy Land," where bushes burst into flame, where rocks and volcanoes gushed sacred metaphors and the stars bespoke God's grandeur. No longer. The supernatural world has seemingly gone into hiding, leaving us alone with the visible. The thirst for God, though, for *contact* with the unseen, the hunger for love from a cosmic Parent who can somehow fashion meaning from this scrambled world, defiantly persists.

God is personal. The Bible, both Old Testament and New, portrays a God who affects us and is affected by us. "For the Lord takes delight in his people," says the psalmist (149:4); at times God also takes great exception to his people, say the prophets. The personality of God leaps out of almost every page of the Bible. "God is love," says the apostle John. "Whoever lives in love lives in God, and God in him." It would be difficult to get more personal.

Why, then, do we find it so difficult to relate personally to this God? At various times people tended to pray to local saints, who seemed more accessible and less scary. Protestant Reformers and Catholic mystics, though, challenged us to relate to God directly, without intermediaries. And modern evangelicalism summons us to know God, to talk to God in conversational language, to love God as one might love a friend. Listen to the "praise songs" in modern churches, which sound exactly like love songs played on pop radio, with God or Jesus substituted as the lover.

Do we, like billboards for Pepsi, fan a thirst we cannot quench? Just last week my church sang: "I want to know you more / I want to touch you / I want to see your face." Nowhere in the Bible do I find a promise that we will touch God, or see his face, not in this life at least.

Modern American religion speaks in "friendly" terms with God even though, as C. S. Lewis points out in *The Four Loves*, friendship is the form of love that least accurately describes the truth of a creature's encounter with the Creator. How, then, can we have a "personal relationship" with a God who is invisible, when we're never quite sure he's there?

ENCOUNTERING GOD THROUGH THOSE IN THE BIBLE (3 – 5 MINUTES)

Read Psalm 42:1–11. If you are reading in a group, choose two readers to alternate as follows, representing each part of the psalmist's self.

Reader 1: verses 1–4
Reader 2: verses 5–6a
Reader 1: verses 6b–7
Reader 2: verse 8

Reader 1: verses 9–10
Reader 2: verse 11

REACHING FOR GOD WITH OTHERS (20 MINUTES)

If you are in a large group, break into groups of four to six for this discussion time. Introduce yourselves to each other. Tell the others briefly about yourself. Are you single? Married? Do you have children? Do you work outside the home?

1. When you think of the invisibility of God, how do you feel?
   • Crazy. My senses are very important to me. I really struggle in relating to a God I can't see, hear, or touch.
   • Frustrated. I can accept that God is Spirit, but often I can't seem to scale the hurdle of how to get to know this Spirit.
   • Doubtful. God is so vague to me that sometimes I'm not convinced he's really there.
   • Grateful. I struggle at times, but the material world hasn't filled me up. I get more from God as a Spirit than I do from anyone or anything else, despite the challenges.
   • Other:_____

2. Briefly discuss with the group your response to the writer of Psalm 42. Can you readily identify (now or in your past) with Reader 1, the part of the self that longs for God but has trouble finding him? Can you identify with Reader 2, the side of the self that insists on hoping in God, believing he cares?

3. Turn to page 14 in the book, and as you review the paragraphs about Philip's college reunion, tell the group how long you have identified yourself as a Christian. Can you relate to the experience of disillusionment when the heady concepts of Christianity bump up against the realities of daily living? When in your life has this kind of bump

occurred? If you are still exploring Christianity and considering where your beliefs lie, have you experienced any similar disillusionment?

4. Consider the following lines from a letter Philip wrote to God a decade ago (pp. 17–18 in the book).

Occasionally I get caught up in your world, and love you, and I've learned to cope OK in this world, but how do I bring the two together? That's my prayer, I guess: to believe in the possibility of change. Living inside myself, change is hard to observe.... How do I let you change me in my essence, in my nature, to make me more like you? Or is that even possible?

Do you, like Philip, struggle with finding a continuous unity with God and seeing him change you within? Or do you struggle more often with understanding what you see God doing or not doing in the world around you?

5. Philip, on page 19, tells of three respected Christians from past and present who met difficulties in relating to God. Saint Augustine struggled to place absolute trust in an invisible God and an imperfect church. Author Hannah Whitall Smith *(The Christian's Secret of a Happy Life)* experienced distress because of an unfaithful husband and children who left the faith. Author Eugene Peterson, as an adolescent, observed "Spirit-filled" hypocritical Christians. How do you feel as you read about the struggles of these spiritual leaders?

• Surprised. I thought there were some people who just believed God and never doubted.
• Unsettled. I have so far to go in my walk with God. If these spiritual giants couldn't "arrive," I don't think there's any hope for me.
• Tentative. I feel Yancey is bending their stories to fit his theme. These leaders struggled, but it was through their struggles that they gained the wisdom and perspective to impact many.

REACHING FOR THE INVISIBLE GOD STUDY GUIDE

- Relieved. These stories are a reminder to me that I can keep progressing in my relationship with God despite my doubts.
- Other:_____

6. Review the story of the Russian Orthodox priest on pages 25–27 in the book. Brother Bonifato performed a series of time-consuming formalities in a Russian prison chapel in order to offer a prayer, requested spontaneously, for the prisoners. Some complain that in Russia God seems far away and unapproachable to the individual, due to these formalities. Yet Thomas Merton said, "If you find God with great ease, perhaps it is not God that you have found." What do you think? Talk about your own church. Does it seem formal or casual to you? Is God approachable? Is contact with God *too* easy?

7. C. S. Lewis wrote, "There comes a moment when the children who have been playing at burglars hush suddenly: was that a *real* footstep in the hall? There comes a moment when people who have been dabbling in religion . . . suddenly draw back. Supposing we really found Him? We never meant it to come to *that!* Worse still, supposing He had found us?" (p. 28). Can you tell about a time when you felt what Philip calls a "tug" from God?

Philip writes, "Nowhere in the Bible do I find a promise that we will touch God, or see his face, not in this life at least." Quoting C. S. Lewis, Philip adds, "Friendship is the form of love that least accurately describes the truth of a creature's encounter with the Creator" (pp. 32–33). Considering the times you have felt a tug from God, how do you respond to these statements?

GRASPING FOR UNDERSTANDING OF MYSELF, MY GOD (10–20 MINUTES OR MORE)

As we explore the seeming gulf between ourselves and God, it is helpful to know that each of us will experience unique struggles due to our life experiences, personality, spiritual growth, expectations, and other characteristics that make us who we are. In seeking greater peace and depth in our relationship with God, it helps to look at various aspects of ourselves and of God, just as we would do with another person in a troubled marriage or friendship. This examination of underlying perspectives will help us gain a true picture of spiritual life and will change how we relate to God.

You may choose to reflect on the following questions either together as a small group during this session or in personal time at home during the coming week. It's very helpful, if time permits, to share about these experiences with others in the group. As we listen to one another, we realize that our struggles and differing perspectives are impacted greatly by our unique life circumstances. In gaining new understanding of one another, we can gain new understanding of God.

In this session we will consider the overall life experiences that have brought us to where we stand today with God. Reflect on these questions:

- How would you describe the spiritual atmosphere in which you grew up?
- What was it that drew you to God?
- What have been the outstanding times of trial in your life?
- In what ways did God seem present or absent in your trials?

CLINGING TO GOD DESPITE THE DISTANCE (5–10 MINUTES)

In this section of each study, we will take a few minutes to be silent together before God and open ourselves to meaningful contact with him. This time may include prayer, meditation on a verse of Scripture or a meaningful quotation about God, or writing thoughts or prayers in a journal. Consider bringing a notebook or journal to each session, or you can write in the space provided. You may not be accustomed to spending time in silence before God, or you may not have experienced doing this in the presence of a group. Try to push through any level of discomfort you may feel. The discomfort will recede in time, and you will find this to be an important part of your time together and with God.

Today let's spend a few minutes meditating on, or quietly thinking about, the following prayer of Anselm of Canterbury.

> I do desire to understand a little of your Truth which my heart already believes and loves. I do not seek to understand so that I may believe, but I do believe so that I may understand; and what is more, I believe that unless I do believe I shall not understand.

As you sit before God, close your eyes or simply bow your head. Your prayer may be that of Anselm. Or you may need to pray, as did one New Testament follower of Jesus (and many since), "I do believe; help me overcome my unbelief!" (Mark 9:24).

LONGING FOR GOD IN THE WEEK AHEAD (OPTIONAL)

You can integrate this study into your life throughout the week by using the following suggestions and readings.

- Consider gathering together as a group sometime this week and watching the movie *Contact* with Jodie Foster. After the movie, discuss: What parallels do you find between Foster's pursuit of life from another world and our pursuit of God? What parallels or differences do you find in the outcome of Foster's search and the outcome of your own?
- Reflect on these psalms in the week ahead as your time allows.
  Day 1: Psalm 13
  Day 2: Psalm 61
  Day 3: Psalm 63
  Day 4: Psalm 77
  Day 5: Psalm 143

DOUBT AND DIFFICULTIES

———◦◦◦———

The excerpt below is from *Reaching for the Invisible God*.

I must exercise faith simply to believe that God exists, a basic requirement for any relationship. And yet when I wish to explore how faith works, I usually sneak in by the back door of doubt, for I best learn about my own need for faith during its absence. God's invisibility guarantees I will experience times of doubt.

Everyone dangles on a pendulum that swings from belief to unbelief, back to belief, and ends—where? Some never find faith. Others have faith, then lose it.

I feel kinship with those who find it impossible to believe or find it impossible to keep on believing in the face of apparent betrayal. I have been in a similar place at times, and I marvel that God bestowed on me an unexpected gift of faith. Examining my own periods of faithlessness, I see in them all manner of unbelief. Sometimes I shy away for lack of evidence, sometimes I slink away in hurt or disillusionment, and sometimes I turn aside in willful disobedience. Something, though, keeps drawing me back to God. What? I ask myself.

"This is a hard teaching. Who can accept it?" said Jesus' disciples in words that resonate in every doubter. Jesus' listeners found themselves simultaneously attracted and repelled, like a compass needle brought close to a magnet. As his words sank in, one by one the crowd of onlookers and followers slouched away, leaving only the Twelve. "You do not want to leave too, do you?" Jesus asked them in a tone somewhere between plaintiveness and resignation. As usual, Simon Peter spoke up: "Lord, to whom shall we go?"

That, for me, is the bottom-line answer to why I stick around. To my shame, I admit that one of the strongest reasons I stay in the fold is the lack of good alternatives, many of which I have tried. *Lord, to whom shall I go?* The only thing more difficult than having a relationship with an invisible God is having no such relationship.

———— ❧ ————

Doubt is the skeleton in the closet of faith, and I know no better way to treat a skeleton than to bring it into the open and expose it for what it is: not something to hide or fear, but a hard structure on which living tissue may grow. If I asked every person to stop reading whose faith has wavered, I might as well end the book with this sentence. Why, then, does the church treat doubt as an enemy? Doubt always coexists with faith, for in the presence of certainty who would need faith at all?

———— ❧ ————

Although we cannot control doubt, which often creeps up on us uninvited, we can learn to channel it in ways that make doubt more likely to be nourishing than toxic. For starters, I try to approach my doubts with the humility appropriate to my creaturely status.

———— ❧ ————

Ask a strong, stable family where they got such strength, and you may very well hear a story of crisis. Relationships gain strength when they are stretched to the breaking point and do not break. Seeing this principle lived out among people, I can better understand one of the mysteries of relating to God. Faith boils down to a question of trust in a given relationship. Do I have confidence in my loved ones—or in God, as the case may be? If I do stand on a bedrock of trust, the worst of circumstances will not destroy the relationship.

One Christian thinker, Søren Kierkegaard, spent a lifetime exploring the tests of faith that call into question God's trustworthiness. Again and again he turned to biblical characters like Job and Abraham, who survived excruciating trials of faith. During their times of testing, it appeared to both Job and Abraham that God was contradicting himself. *God surely would not act in such a way—yet clearly he is.* Kierkegaard ultimately concluded that the purest faith emerges from just such an ordeal. Even though I do not understand, I will trust God regardless.

———— ❧ ————

Having examined every instance of human suffering recorded in the Bible, I have come away convinced that many Christians who face a trial of faith attempt to answer a different question than God is asking. By instinct we flee to the questions that look backward in time: What caused this tragedy? Was God involved? What is God trying to tell me? We judge the relationship on such incomplete evidence.

The Bible gives many examples of suffering that, like Job's, have nothing to do with God's punishment. Not once did Jesus counsel someone to accept suffering as God's will; rather he went about healing illness and disability.

The Bible supplies no systematic answers to the "Why?" questions and often avoids them entirely. A flat tire, a backed-up sink, a case of laryngitis—these tests, however minor, may well provoke a crisis of trust in our relationship with God. Yet we dare not tread into areas God has sealed off as his domain. Divine providence is a mystery that only God understands, and belongs in what I have called "The Encyclopedia of Theological Ignorance" for a simple reason: no time-bound human, living on a rebellious planet, blind to the realities of the unseen world, has the ability to comprehend such answers—God's reply to Job in a nutshell.

———— ❧ ————

Many Christians quote the verse Romans 8:28, "And we know that in all things God works for the good of those who love him," with the implication that somehow everything will turn out for the best. The Greek original text is more properly translated, "In everything that happens, God works for good with those who love him." That promise, I have found to hold true in all the disasters and hardships I have known personally. Things happen, some of them good, some of them bad, many of them beyond our control. In all these things, I have felt the reliable constant of a God willing to work with me and through me to produce something good. Faith in such a process will, I'm convinced, always be rewarded, even though the "Why?" questions go unanswered.

————

For many people, it takes the jolt of tragedy, illness, or death to create an existential crisis of faith. At such a moment, we want clarity; God wants our trust. A Scottish preacher in the last century lost his wife suddenly, and after her death he preached an unusually personal sermon. He admitted in the message that he did not understand this life of ours. But still less could he understand how people facing loss could abandon faith. "Abandon it for what!" he said. "You people in the sunshine may believe the faith, but we in the shadow *must* believe it. We have nothing else."

ENCOUNTERING GOD THROUGH THOSE IN THE BIBLE (3–5 MINUTES)

Read Genesis 22:1–18.

REACHING FOR GOD WITH OTHERS (25 MINUTES)

If you are in a large group, break into groups of four to six for this discussion time. Introduce yourselves to each other if necessary. Briefly share with the others about one of the biggest risks you have ever taken. Maybe bungee jumping, or getting married, or moving to a new city without knowing anyone, or quitting a job before you'd secured another. How did you feel as you took this risk?

1. Consider the story of Abraham climbing the mountain to sacrifice Isaac. What do you think enabled him to make this climb? Did he understand why God was asking him to sacrifice Isaac? Why would God ask such a difficult thing of him in the first place? If you know anything about Abraham's prior life, can you remember whether he always acted in such absolute faith?

Philip writes on pages 37 and 38, "Everyone dangles on a pendulum that swings from belief to unbelief, back to belief, and ends—where?" and "Examining my own periods of faithlessness, I see in them all manner of unbelief. Sometimes I shy away for lack of evidence, sometimes I slink away in hurt or disillusionment, and sometimes I turn aside in willful disobedience. Something, though, keeps drawing me back to God."

Reflect on your own pendulum of belief. Do you swing between belief and unbelief weekly or daily (even hourly), or do you look back to see larger blocks of time in which you swung between the two? (Please share as honestly as you are able. Recognize that we will all vary greatly in the form belief has taken in our lives. Through this sharing, we will all deepen our relationship with God and each other.)

2. Review Philip's story on page 39 about the prayer vigil in his Chicago church. Senior citizens from a housing project were the most enthusiastic participants, staying all night. "We got time and we got faith," they said. "Some of us don't sleep much anyway. We can pray all night if needs be." Do you know anyone who has this kind of child-like faith, despite difficult circumstances in his or her life? Do you agree that it seems "faith appears where least expected and falters where it should be thriving"?

Philip speculates on whether people naturally divide into various "faith types" just as they divide into personality types (pp. 40–41). "We are not all shy or melancholic or introverted; why should we expect to have the same measure or kind of faith?" What do you think of this idea?

If you were to describe your own faith type, what would it be? Consider the following, or modify these to describe yourself more accurately.

- *Persistent skeptic.* I can't let go of belief in the core of my being, but I think I'll always spend more time questioning God and doubting his provision than trusting. Like Yancey in the past, I feel a lot of guilt over my lack of faith.
- *Hopeful skeptic.* Something in me leans pretty regularly toward skepticism with God and his work in my life. But I don't feel stuck there. I'm usually able to step back from my skepticism and move toward a more faith-filled approach. I feel God is helping me to gradually change my patterns of response.
- *Persistent believer.* I haven't had any serious doubt for a long time. I trust God with everything, mostly because I know I can't really trust anybody else. I hurt for those who struggle in believing God, because in good times and bad he has always been there for me.
- *Hopeful believer.* Mine has been a real journey of faith. I didn't always have explicit trust in God. It's taken some very difficult times in my life to build my faith and teach me that no matter what, God is good and will always care for me and my circumstances.

3. Philip says, "In my case, doubt has prompted me to question many things that needed questioning and also to investigate alternatives to faith, none of which measure up. I remain a Christian today due to my doubts" (p. 43). Then he notes that sometimes doubt can lead a person away from faith. Do you know anyone close to you, perhaps a family member, who has lost his or her faith due to doubt? What were the circumstances?

DOUBT AND DIFFICULTIES

What role have you found humility to play in your life when doubts arise (pp. 43–44)? Do you agree with Philip that "our approach to difficult issues should befit our status as finite creatures"? What does he mean?

4. How do you respond to the following words by Philip: "Churches that leave room for mystery, that do not pretend to spell out what God himself has not spelled out, create an environment most conducive to worship" (pp. 46–47)? Are you content to allow some mystery in your faith and your relationship with God, or do you feel compelled to have an answer for all questions that arise, both for yourself and for others (new Christians, children, believers of other denominations, nonbelievers)?

Jesus appeared to "doubting Thomas" and gently solved his doubt issues. However, Thomas saw Jesus only because Thomas was still welcomed into the company of disciples. Jesus tended to appear only to groups of believers after his resurrection. The willingness of the other disciples, who knew Thomas was mistaken, to allow him in their midst was what put him in the place where Jesus could reveal himself to Thomas. Is your church a "safe place for doubt"? Do friends and family members who doubt feel safe with you?

5. Read the quote by George Everett Ross on pages 52–53. Think about one of the most difficult periods of your life. Did you lean closer to the first kind of faith or the second? How did you make it through this trial as a result?

27

6. Before reading this book, what has been your perspective on God's involvement in things like flat tires, clogged sinks, hard-to-find parking places, and untimely chest colds? Does God have a hand in these? Or does he reserve his involvement for the more important and spiritual areas of your life? (Note that individuals in the group may have widely varying opinions on this issue. If so, listen carefully to each other, and have a lively discussion!)

What do you think of the idea of viewing God's interaction as an underground river, an abiding presence from below, rather than an overhead bolt of lightning (pp. 58–59)?

7. Have you ever questioned whether a particular trial in your life was God's punishment for your sin? Have you realized any blessing in your life through this trial? Have you sensed God changing your perspective from a focus on the "why" of your trial to a focus on his weaving of good amid the pain?

Do you have any prayer needs to share with the group?

GRASPING FOR UNDERSTANDING OF MYSELF, MY GOD (10–20 MINUTES OR MORE)

Today we will spend more time reflecting on our individual faith types and asking God to help us better understand our own perspectives. Glance back at the faith types listed in question 2, and think about how you identified yourself. Consider:

- How do your prior and current life experiences contribute to the type of faith you hold today?
- How much of your faith is built upon conscious choices you make?
- How much has your faith type changed in past years or months?

Again this week you may choose to reflect on these questions either at home during personal time or now with your group. Any group sharing that is possible will help us all to understand ourselves better. It is enlightening to see that others don't always respond the way we do. As we better understand others' lives and relationships with God, we gain wisdom for our own lives.

CLINGING TO GOD DESPITE THE DISTANCE (5 – 10 MINUTES)

Now we will take a few minutes to be silent together before God. As you close your eyes, lay your hands open on your lap with palms up. Present yourself to God, explaining to him your understanding of your level of faith, or your faith type. Don't feel a need to confess the inadequacies of your faith. Simply speak to God in honesty. Then, in humility, ask God to take your faith in its current form and mold and shape it as he desires. Ask that he would bring peace.

You may not know your group well and may feel uncomfortable with silence, but try to view this corporate time with God as a gift to each other as well as to God. It is a time in which as one group, accepting and supporting one another, we offer our faltering selves to God. This time in itself can become a step of faith.

LONGING FOR GOD IN THE WEEK AHEAD (OPTIONAL)

You can integrate this study into your life throughout the week by using the following suggestions and readings.

- Pay special attention this week to the small and big events happening in your life. Can you see God's involvement in any way?
- Reflect on these Bible passages in the week ahead as your time allows.

Day 1: Job 1:6–22
Day 2: Job 3:1–26
Day 3: Job 42:1–17
Day 4: Habakkuk 1:1–7; 3:16–19
Day 5: John 9:1–7

The following excerpt is taken from the journal *First Things*, about the author Peter De Vries, whom Philip refers to on pages 37–38 of his book. Don't let the first sentence discourage you from reading this somewhat academic yet valuable reflection!

Peter De Vries' novels give fictional life to the disbelief that eschews oleaginous substitutes. I am not here claiming De Vries to be a Christian in what he affirmed, only in what he negated—namely, in his refusal to be cozily consoled when the children were no more [as the Old Testament Rachel refused to be consoled]. Many of De Vries' readers know that his most celebrated novel, *The Blood of the Lamb* (1962), has autobiographical origins. Both De Vries' sister and his own daughter died young. After his sister's death, he once told me, his mother refused ever again to sing in church. Yet their minister, in making a pastoral call, had the gall to inquire about her silence, failing to see that this Dutch-immigrant mother was a latter-day Rachel, refusing to be comforted by anyone but God—and perhaps not even by him. De Vries lets his mother's voice be heard when his narrator, Don Wanderhope, loses his own brother to pneumonia. In the novel as in life, a minister has come to proffer the hope that Wanderhope knows to be bogus. He will not take solace in a God whose sovereignty makes him the direct cause of every occurrence, both human and natural. Hence Wanderhope's poignant wail of disbelief:

> My sensation, rather than fear or piety, was a baffled and uncomprehending rage. That flesh with which I had lain in comradely embrace [was] destroyable, on such short notice, by a whim known as divine? ... Who wantonly scattered such charm, who broke such flesh like bread for his purposes?

When Wanderhope's own daughter Carol dies of leukemia at age eleven, his disbelief is no longer partial but total. He refuses to find any relief in the notion that her death is the work of God's beneficent will. Instead, he engages in his own willful inversion of the central Christian claims. It is not Christ who is slain from the foundation of the world for the sins of the world, but little Carol herself who is the innocent creature needlessly destroyed. The fountain filled with blood has been drawn not from Emmanuel's but from this helpless child's veins. Wanderhope thus addresses the dying Carol as his "lamb," and he strokes her hair as "precious fleece." He describes her needle marks and incisions as "stigmata." Carol dies at the very hour when the other children are frolicking their way home from school, even as it is also the hour of Christ's death: three o'clock in the afternoon. The abandonment that occurred at Calvary may not have been the great act of substitutionary atonement wrought by God in Christ, De Vries suggests, but a fearful sign of God's perpetual truancy amidst human anguish.

One wonders whether De Vries the ex-Calvinist might have been rescued from such horrible fears if he had been taught a doctrine of divine sovereignty that did not insist on God's omnicausality. Calvin chose his adjective carefully when he declared that "All events are governed by God's secret plan." That God's providential will for the world is not transparent but hidden from human sight requires that we walk by faith, that we struggle through the valley of doubt as well as the shadow of death. Yet if God's work were completely concealed, human history and individual life would be random and rudderless, the chaotic product of an accidental universe. Both Catholic Scholasticism and Protestant Orthodoxy sought to steer a middle course between such false notions of divine transparency and divine opacity by insisting on the distinction between first and second causes. God's primary will does indeed superintend the working of all things together for good (Romans 8:28). Yet there are secondary causes—both natural and human, at once free and contingent and necessary—that may temporarily deflect even if they do not finally defeat God's providence. Sentimental Christianity spurns this distinction, trying instead to make evident the God who remains hidden even in his incarnation. It encourages either cozy feelings of assurance that the Lord makes everything work to our benefit, or else cozy communities assured that they are God's only hands and feet in the work of peace and justice. Christian disbelief disavows both sentimentalities.

Even with sentimentalism set aside, we are still left to deal with the terrible death of Carol Wanderhope. In the scene that follows it, De Vries hints at the one true way to avoid the twin evils of divine omnicausality and godless accidentality. Don Wanderhope had bought a cake for Carol's birthday, but he had inadvertently left it in the Catholic church where, on the way to the hospital, he had stopped to say one last desperate prayer for her recovery. Staggering both from grief and from the liquor he has drunk to numb it, Don remembers the cake. He returns to the church to get it. In a gesture of pure metaphysical fury, Wanderhope flings the confection in the face of the crucifix hanging over the church door. Yet just as Jeremiah hears God answering the inconsolable Rachel, so does De Vries reveal a strange solace in this act of defiance. A bleary-eyed Wanderhope sees Christ wiping the icing from his eyes "very slowly, very deliberately, with infinite patience. . . . Then the cheeks were wiped down with the same sense of grave and gentle ritual, with all the kind sobriety of one whose voice could be heard saying, 'Suffer the little children to come unto me . . . for such is the kingdom of heaven.'"

Just as Jacob wrestles with the angel all night until he has been blessed, even if his battle with God leaves him permanently lamed; as Jeremiah protests that God absconds behind the blank wall of Israel's exile; as the Psalmist laments that the wicked prosper while the faithful and the righteous languish; as Koheleth [the "teacher" of Ecclesiastes] complains that life is a great weariness under a sun that also rises and also goes down without producing anything new; as Job angrily contends with the God who has subjected him to unspeakable suffering without due cause; even as Rachel mourns in Ramah that her children are no more—so does Peter De Vries have his characters decline all comfort that is not real comfort. Don Wanderhope refuses to believe that his daughter's death is either the mechanical execution of a divine plan or the random result of godless chance. His encounter with the cake-splattered Christ suggests, instead, that God has strangely subjected himself to the sin and rage of his people. This is indeed a dark revelation, and De Vries claimed to be no more than a backslidden unbeliever. Yet his fiction makes powerful witness against the soggy spirituality of our age, confronting us with a Cross which demands our disbelief in all sentimental substitutes.[1]

FAITH THAT WORKS

The excerpt below is from *Reaching for the Invisible God*.

A paranoid person orients life around fear. I am learning that mature faith, which encompasses both simple faith and fidelity, works the opposite of paranoia. It reassembles all the events of life around trust in a loving God. When good things happen, I accept them as gifts from God, worthy of thanksgiving. When bad things happen, I do not take them as necessarily sent by God—I see evidence in the Bible to the contrary—and I find in them no reason to divorce God. Rather, I trust that God can use even those bad things for my benefit. That, at least, is the goal toward which I strive.

A faithful person sees life from the perspective of trust, not fear. Bedrock faith allows me to believe that, despite the chaos of the present moment, God does reign; that regardless of how worthless I may feel, I truly matter to a God of love; that no pain lasts forever and no evil triumphs in the end. Faith sees even the darkest deed of all history, the death of God's Son, as a necessary prelude to the brightest.

Many things happen in this world that are clearly against God's will. Read the prophets, God's designated spokesmen, who thunder against idolatry, injustice, violence, and other symptoms of human sin and rebellion. Read the Gospel accounts, where Jesus upsets the religious establishment by freeing people from disabilities the divines had deemed "God's will." Providence may be a great mystery, nonetheless I find no justification for blaming God for what God so clearly opposes.

The skeptic's question does not melt away, though. How can I praise God for the good things in life without censuring him for the bad? I can do so only by establishing an attitude of trust—paranoia in reverse—based on what I have learned in relationship with God.

Over time, both through personal experience and my study of the Bible, I have come to know certain qualities of God. God's style often baffles me: he moves at a slow pace, prefers rebels and prodigals, restrains his power, and speaks in whispers and silence. Yet even in these qualities I see evidence of his longsuffering, mercy, and desire to woo rather than compel. When in doubt, I focus on Jesus, the most unfiltered revelation of God's own self. I have learned to trust God, and when some tragedy or evil occurs that I cannot synthesize with the God I have come to know and love, then I look to other explanations.

Gregory of Nicea once called St. Basil's faith "ambidextrous" because he welcomed pleasures with the right hand and afflictions with the left, convinced that both would serve God's design for him. Here is what ambidextrous, or "two-handed" faith means to me, in theory if not always in practice. I take "everything without exception" as God's action in the sense of asking what I can learn from it and praying for God to redeem it by improving me. I take nothing as God's action in the sense of judging God's character, for I have learned to accept my puny status as a creature—which includes a limited point of view that obscures unseen forces in the present as well as a future known only to God. The skeptic may insist this unfairly lets God off the hook, but perhaps that's what faith is: trusting God's goodness despite any apparent evidence against it. As a soldier trusts his general's orders; better, as a child trusts her loving parent.

My pastor in Chicago, Bill Leslie, said he often felt like an old hand-operated water pump, the kind still found in some campgrounds. Everyone who came to him for help would pump vigorously a few times, and each time he felt something drain out of him. Ultimately he reached a place of spiritual emptiness, with nothing more to give. He felt dry, desiccated.

In the midst of this period, Bill went on a weeklong retreat and bared his soul to his assigned spiritual director, a nun. He expected her to offer soothing words about what a sacrificial, unselfish person he was, or perhaps recommend a sabbatical. Instead she said, "Bill, there's only one thing to do if your reservoir runs dry. You've got to go deeper." He returned from that retreat convinced that his faith depended less on his outer journey of life and ministry than on his inner journey toward spiritual depth.

The Bible makes no rosy promises about living only in springtime. Instead, it points toward faith that helps us prepare for arid seasons. Harsh winters will come, followed by scorching summers. Yet if the roots of faith go deep enough, tapping into Living Water, we can survive the drought times and flourish in times of plenty.

———— ◅∽► ————

According to Stanley Hauerwas, the life of faith consists of patience and hope. When something comes along to test our relationship with God, we rely on those two virtues: patience formed by a long memory, and hope that our faithfulness will prove worth the risk. Jews and Christians have always emphasized these virtues, Hauerwas notes, for we believe that a God who is both good and faithful controls the universe; patience and hope keep faith alive during times that cast doubt on that belief.

I would paraphrase Hauerwas by saying the life of faith consists of living in the past and in the future. I live in the past in order to ground myself in what God has already done, as a way of gaining confidence in what he might do again. Relating to an invisible God involves certain handicaps: with no sensory evidence in the present, we must look backward to remind ourselves of who it is we are relating to. Every time God introduced himself as "the God of Abraham, Isaac, and Jacob," he reminded his chosen people of his history with them—a history that for all three forebears included seasons of testing and doubt.

New Testament letters advise the same: Study the Scriptures diligently, as necessary road maps for contests of faith. Beyond the Bible, the testimony of the entire church bears witness of God's faithfulness. Where would my own faith be, I wonder, without Augustine, Donne, Dostoevski, Jürgen Moltmann, Thomas Merton, C. S. Lewis? Many times I have leaned on their words as an exhausted traveler might lean against a roadside monument.

Although I do not keep a formal journal, my writings accomplish something similar. I pick up an article I wrote twenty-five years ago and marvel at the passion I felt over an issue I have hardly thought about since. Such anger, doubt, barely controlled cynicism! I find cries of lament penciled long ago in the margins of my Bible and give thanks that I made it through that particular valley. When exuberant, I look at my past writings and am shocked at the sloughs of despond I wallowed in; when depressed, I am shocked at the bright faith I used to have. Mainly, from the past I gain perspective that what I feel and believe right now I will not always feel and believe—which drives me to sink roots deeper, into layers of subsoil unaffected by El Niño or other vagaries of climate.

⁃⁓⁃

Thomas Merton found the secret to true freedom: If we live to please God alone, we set ourselves free from the cares and worries that press in on us. So many of my own cares trace back to concern over other people: whether I measure up to their expectations, whether they find me desirable. Living for God alone involves a radical reorientation, a stripping away of anything that might lure me from the primary goal of pleasing God. Living in faith involves me pleasing God, far more than God pleasing me.

⁃⁓⁃

"The motions of Grace; the hardness of heart; external circumstances," Pascal jotted down in one of his cryptic notes. These three things encompass our lives. External circumstances press in: family strife, job pressures, financial worries, global concerns. The motions of grace, God's gifts within, seek to ground us in a deeper reality. Hardness of heart? Of the three, this alone falls somewhat under my control. All I can do is pray daily for God to "batter my heart," in John Donne's phrase, or better yet, to melt it with his love.

ENCOUNTERING GOD THROUGH THOSE IN THE BIBLE (3–5 MINUTES)

Read the following Scripture passages.
Psalm 139:7–12
Jeremiah 17:7–8
Philippians 4:11–13
Romans 8:28–32, 35–39

Reaching for God with Others (25 minutes)

If you are in a large group, break into groups of four to six for this discussion time. Introduce yourselves to each other if necessary. Briefly share with the others: Do you suffer from any phobias, such as claustrophobia, arachnophobia, fear of flying, or fear of heights?

1. Have you ever known a paranoid person or even a severely depressed person—one who assumed the worst would always happen and distrusted everyone? How often was this person right? Do you have any idea why this person lived in so much fear?

   Look at the paragraphs on page 65 about paranoia and mature faith. Philip writes that mature faith works the opposite of paranoia. "It reassembles all the events of life around trust in a loving God." Although we may not be paranoid people overall, most of us have flashes of paranoia occasionally. Consider those times when you have been gripped with excessive or unnecessary fear (staying home alone at night, preparing for an airplane trip, considering why a friend has not returned a call, decisions about a child, fear about losing a job). What effect might deeper faith have on these flashes of fear?

   How does Psalm 139:7–12 speak to these times of fear?

   See the note at the bottom of page 67 about the passage in Daniel 10 and the spiritual battle that occurred in response to Daniel's prayer. What does this story suggest about the role of prayer in fearful situations?

2. Review the illustration on page 67 of a spy who loses contact with his home country. What do you think the spy feels like, alone in enemy territory and without communication with his own country? Does his trust in his country remove his feelings of loneliness? Of fear? Why does trust in his home country keep him from assuming they have failed him? Obviously, not many of us are put in this extreme position, but have you ever had an experience of loneliness and fear that resembled such a state?

See the quote on page 68 by C. S. Lewis. How do Lewis's words influence your perspective on faith and how much you can trust God?

3. Philip talks on page 69 about "ambidextrous" faith, which welcomes pleasures with the right hand and afflictions with the left, believing both will serve God's design. What is your reaction to the idea of ambidextrous faith?

   • It's unnatural! This is spiritual pie-in-the-sky thinking. It may sound good, but can anyone truly see suffering this way? I'd still rather God take away my trials.

   • More guilt. I suppose this is the way I should see the good and the bad in my life, but I don't automatically hold this view. It's one more reason to feel guilty about my lack of faith.

   • Yes, but. . . . I believe this fully in my mind, but I still fall apart when hard times hit. Why am I unable to transfer what I believe from my mind to my heart?

   • I'm closer to this outlook than ever before in my life. I doubt painful times will ever be easy for me, but I'm finally coming to a place where I believe in God's goodness toward me even when I'm hurting.

4. If all in your group have not read chapter 5 in the book, consider reading now, if time allows, the story of John Donne, beginning on page 70 with, "I think also of John Donne ..." and concluding at the end of the chapter. Consider the familiar lines "Never send to know for whom the bell tolls; it tolls for thee." Before reading this book, what have been your thoughts on death? Are you afraid of death? Have thoughts or fears of dying been a regular part of your life? If you were seriously ill, as Donne was, do you think you would have similar questions and struggles?

How does Romans 8:28–32, 35–39 speak to our concerns about death?

5. Review Philip's story of Pastor Bill Leslie on page 73. Have you ever considered the necessity of a deep and mature faith while experiencing a personal crisis? When have you been grateful during a difficult time for the depth of faith you do have? Has such a crisis ever helped you develop a deeper faith?

Reread Jeremiah 17:7–8. Do you see yourself as the tree described here? Do you feel that your roots right now are shallow or deep? Why is it wise to seek deep spiritual growth before hard times hit? Is it possible to grow deeper while undergoing a hard time?

6. Philip relates Stanley Hauerwas's view that "the life of faith consists of patience and hope ... patience formed by a long memory, and hope that our faithfulness will prove worth the risk." Are you usually patient or impatient when trials hit? Do you normally feel hopeful or hopeless when all around you is dark? What experiences, if any, do you look back on to remind yourself of God's goodness and to strengthen your patience?

How do you respond to Philip's words "Mainly, from the past I gain perspective that what I feel and believe right now I will not always feel and believe"? Is this perspective something you have struggled with?

7. Review the story of Nelson Mandela on pages 78–79 and the words of Philippians 4:11–13. Most of us have not had to learn contentment in circumstances such as Mandela's, yet we've all had periods when life was less than ideal. During such times, did you seek contentment in the midst of your situation, or did you focus primarily on grieving and changing your circumstances?

Review the paragraphs about Thomas Merton on page 82. Do you agree that modern city life encourages worries about money, status, and control? Have you found it possible to turn your back on these worries and focus on pleasing God alone? Can you share any insights on how you have made progress in doing this?

Do you have any prayer needs to share with the group?

GRASPING FOR UNDERSTANDING OF MYSELF, MY GOD (10–20 MINUTES OR MORE)

Psychology tells us that fear is at the root of many emotions, including anger, jealousy, and pride. In seeking to gain control of unwanted emotions, we must first understand the fears that prompt them. As we obtain a proper perspective on our fears, the unwanted emotions become transformed, allowing honesty and a more mature perspective to take their place.

Likewise, fear plays an important role in the spiritual life. It sits at the base of a crippled or immature faith. In dealing with our fears as related to trusting God, it helps to better understand them and then to see how true knowledge of God makes them unnecessary. As we seek, with God's help, to send the roots of faith deeper and wider, fear loses its stronghold.

Spend some time examining your fears. What type of fear plagues you most?

- Fear about my physical safety or death
- Fear that I will not have emotionally fulfilling relationships
- Fear that I will not have a great enough influence in this world
- Fear about financial security
- Fear that I will miss out on the pleasures of life
- Fear that I will not be respected
- Fear that my pain will never heal
- Fear that I will never become the person God wants me to be

Now consider: Does fear have something to do with how much faith and trust you have in God? If your faith grew stronger, would your fears shrink? Depending on the time available, you may choose to reflect on these questions either at home during personal time or now with your group.

CLINGING TO GOD DESPITE THE DISTANCE (5–10 MINUTES)

Now we will take a few minutes to be silent together before God, asking him to help us sink our roots of faith deeper. Read the verses from Jeremiah below, and then close your eyes and imagine yourself standing strong and firm, like a tree planted near the water, with long, sturdy roots. Ask God to increase your faith, making you ever more like this tree.

Blessed is the man who trusts in the Lord, whose confidence is in him. He will be like a tree planted by the water that sends out its roots by the stream. It does not fear when heat comes; its leaves are always green.

JEREMIAH 17:7–8

LONGING FOR GOD IN THE WEEK AHEAD (OPTIONAL)

You can integrate this study into your life throughout the week by using the following suggestions and readings.

- Pay special attention this week when you begin to feel anxious. What fear is at the root of your anxiety?
- When you feel fear or anxiety, turn to God with this prayer: "Lord, I trust in you. My confidence is in you."
- Reflect on these Bible passages and the reading in the week ahead as your time allows.
  Day 1: Isaiah 41:10
  Day 2: Psalm 34:4
  Day 3: Matthew 6:25–34
  Day 4: 2 Corinthians 4:7–18
  Day 5: Hebrews 11:1–12:3

The following excerpt is taken from the book *Ruthless Trust* by author and speaker Brennan Manning.

The most brilliant student I ever taught in seminary was a young man named Augustus Gordon. He now lives as a hermit six months each year in a solitary cabin deep in the Smoky Mountains above Liberty, Tennessee. The remaining half-year he travels the country preaching the gospel on behalf of Food for the Poor, a missionary outreach feeding the hungry and homeless in Haiti, Jamaica, and other Caribbean islands.

On a recent visit I asked him, "Gus, could you define the Christian life in a single sentence?" He didn't even blink before responding. "Brennan," he said, "I can define it in a single word: trust."

It has been more than four decades since I was first ambushed by Jesus in a little chapel in the Allegheny Mountains of western

Pennsylvania. After thousands of hours of prayer and meditation over the intervening years, I can state unequivocally that childlike surrender in trust is the defining spirit of authentic discipleship. And I would add that the supreme need in most of our lives is often the most overlooked—namely, the need for an uncompromising trust in the love of God. Furthermore, I would say that, while there are times when it is good to go to God as might a ragged beggar to the King of kings, it is vastly superior to approach God as a little child would approach his or her papa. . . .

When the brilliant ethicist John Kavanaugh went to work for three months at "the house of the dying" in Calcutta, he was seeking a clear answer as to how best to spend the rest of his life. On the first morning there he met Mother Teresa. She asked, "And what can I do for you?" Kavanaugh asked her to pray for him.

"What do you want me to pray for?" she asked. He voiced the request that he had borne thousands of miles from the United States: "Pray that I have clarity."

She said firmly, "No, I will not do that." When he asked her why, she said, "Clarity is the last thing you are clinging to and must let go of." When Kavanaugh commented that she always seemed to have the clarity he longed for, she laughed and said, "I have never had clarity; what I have always had is trust. So I will pray that you trust God."

"We ourselves have known and put our trust in God's love toward ourselves" (1 John 4:16). Craving clarity, we attempt to eliminate the risk of trusting God. Fear of the unknown path stretching ahead of us destroys childlike trust in the Father's active goodness and unrestricted love.

We often presume that trust will dispel the confusion, illuminate the darkness, vanquish the uncertainty, and redeem the times. But the crowd of witnesses in Hebrews 11 testifies that this is not the case. Our trust does not bring final clarity on this earth. It does not still the chaos or dull the pain or provide a crutch. When all else is unclear, the heart of trust says, as Jesus did on the cross, "Into your hands I commit my spirit" (Luke 23:46).[1]

DAILY
FAITH

———— ❧ ————

The excerpt below is from *Reaching for the Invisible God*.

"My teaching is not my own," Jesus said. "It comes from him who sent me. If anyone chooses to do God's will, he will find out whether my teaching comes from God or whether I speak on my own." Note the sequence: Choose to do God's will, and the confidence will later follow. Jesus presents the journey of faith as a personal pilgrimage begun in uncertainty and fragile trust.

Something similar works in my relationship with God. I wish all obedience sprang from an instinctive desire to please God—alas, it does not. For me, the life of faith sometimes consists of *acting as if* the whole thing is true. I assume that God loves me infinitely, that good will conquer evil, that any adversity can be redeemed, though I have no sure confirmation and only rare epiphanies to spur me along the way. I act as if God is a loving Father; I treat my neighbors as if they truly bear God's image; I forgive those who wrong me as if God has forgiven me first.

I must rely on this technique because of the inherent difference between relating to another human and relating to God. I go to the grocery store and run into a neighbor I have not seen for months. *Judy just went through a divorce,* I say to myself, remembering we have not heard from her lately. Seeing Judy prods me to act. I ask about her life, check on her children, maybe invite her to church. "We must get together with Judy and the kids," I tell my wife later that day, recalling the grocery store encounter.

With God, the sequence reverses. I never "see" God. I seldom run into visual clues that remind me of God *unless I am looking*. The act of looking, the pursuit itself, makes possible the encounter. For this reason, Christianity has always insisted that trust and obedience come first, and knowledge follows. Because of that difference, I persevere at spiritual disciplines no matter how I feel. I do this for one main goal, the goal of all spiritual discipline: I want to know God.

The New Testament epistles repeatedly tell us that love for God, which means acting in loving ways toward God, nurtures the relationship and leads toward growth. I do not get to know God, then do his will; I get to know him *by* doing his will. I enter into an active relationship, which means spending time with God, caring about the people he cares about, and following his commands—whether I spontaneously feel like it or not.

How can we obey without certainty, when plagued by doubts? I have concluded that faith *requires* obedience without full knowledge. Like Job, like Abraham, I accept that much lies beyond my finite grasp, and yet I choose to trust God anyhow, humbly accepting my position as a creature whose worth and very life depend upon God's mercy.

Great victories are won when ordinary people execute their assigned tasks—and a faithful person does not debate each day whether he or she is in the mood to follow the sergeant's orders or show up at a boring job. We exercise faith by responding to the task that lies before us, for we have control only over our actions in the present moment.

More often than I would care to admit, doubts gnaw away at me. I wonder about apparent conflicts in the Bible, about suffering and injustice, about the huge gap between the ideals and reality of the Christian life. At such times I plod on, "acting as if" it is true, relying on the habit of belief, praying for the assurance that eventually comes yet never shields me against the doubts' return.

As Andrew Greeley said, "If one wishes to eliminate uncertainty, tension, confusion and disorder from one's life, there is no point in getting mixed up either with Yahweh or with Jesus of Nazareth." I grew up expecting that a relationship with God would bring order, certainty, and a calm rationality to life. Instead, I have discovered that living in faith involves much dynamic tension.

Throughout church history, Christian leaders have shown an impulse to pin everything down, to reduce behavior and doctrine to absolutes that could be answered on a true-false test. Significantly, I do not find this tendency in the Bible. Far from it, I find instead the mystery and uncertainty that characterize any relationship, especially a relationship between a perfect God and fallible human beings.

Quite simply, being human is hazardous to health. Unlike angels, human beings get cancer, lose their jobs, and go hungry. We need a faith that somehow allows the possibility of joy in the midst of suffering as well as realism in the midst of praise.

Faith will always mean believing in what cannot be proven, committing to that of which we can never be sure. A person who lives in faith must proceed on incomplete evidence, trusting in advance what will only make sense in reverse. As Dennis Covington has written, "Mystery is not the absence of meaning, but the presence of more meaning than we can comprehend."

Everyone has an image of God distorted in some way—we must, of course, since God transcends our ability to imagine him. Our experiences of family and church combine with stray hints from literature and movies to determine what image of God we carry around. How, then, do we know the true God?

I know that my relationship with God will not exactly parallel my relationship with human beings, and in some ways will radically differ. Communication between such unequal creatures will inevitably cause confusion and disappointment on both sides. What we humans want out of a relationship may well run at cross-purposes with what God wants. We are profoundly different, God and I, which explains why friendship is not the primary model used in the Bible to describe our relationship. Worship is.

I understand why the Bible so often turns to love and marriage for pictures of the relationship God wants with us. We are not angels lost in perpetual contemplation, but flawed human beings who prove inconstant in our love contract with God as well as with our human partners. My own marriage, which has endured for three decades, is based on an underlying covenant that we both renegotiate daily. Fidelity, not romance, has kept us together. Yes, marriage lives on love, but it is the kind of love that parenthood demands, or Christian discipleship: a gritty decision to go forward, step by step, one foot in front of the other.

For me, much has remained the same since my decision to follow Christ. Some things have grown harder and more complex. Yet, as with marriage, I have found life with God to be far more satisfying. Following Christ was a starting point, a choice of a path to walk down. I am still plodding that same path—for more years even than I have been married. God lives inside me . . . changing me, orienting me, reminding me of my true identity.

ENCOUNTERING GOD THROUGH THOSE IN THE BIBLE (3 – 5 MINUTES)

Read the following Scripture passages.
Psalm 119:33–56
Proverbs 3:1–8

REACHING FOR GOD WITH OTHERS (25 MINUTES)

If you are in a large group, break into groups of four to six for this discussion time. Introduce yourselves to each other if necessary. Briefly share with the others about the most daunting job interview you have experienced. Were you able to sell yourself?

1. When have you most recently found it necessary to feign love or respect for a person for whom you did not feel much love or respect? Maybe he or she was a boss, coworker, family member, or acquaintance. What was this experience like? Did your act make it easier over time to interact with this person?

Consider Psalm 119:33–56. Pay special attention to verses 41, 50, and 56. Is the writer of this psalm living in obedience to God *because* God has delivered him from his troubles, or is he living obediently *in the midst of* his troubles?

The recovery movement has a slogan that urges, "Fake it till you make it." Often we don't feel capable and in control of ourselves, but acting as if we are can move us further in that direction. Philip applies this perspective to the spiritual life: "For me, the life of faith sometimes consists of *acting as if* the whole thing is true." He continues, "I do not get to know God, then do his will; I get to know him *by* doing his will. I enter into an active relationship, which means spending time with God, caring about the people he cares about, and following his commands—whether I spontaneously feel like it or not" (pp. 88–90).

How does this approach to faith strike you?

- It's a new idea that initially makes me uncomfortable. I believe in acting honestly at all times. I don't think I can turn off my brain in order to follow God.
- It makes me nervous. I know too many people who do the right things for God but never seem to grow more intimate with him.
- Hhmmm. It's a catchy idea. It would be a relief to me to quiet my questions for a while and simply live out my faith, albeit a tentative faith.
- It sounds like what I've been doing for a while now. I've learned that God is reliable, while my feelings often are not. I've seen time and again that when I ignore or downplay God's words, I'm the one who suffers. When I "trust and obey," as the children's song goes, enlightenment often follows.

2. Review the paragraph about Ignatius Loyola on page 91. Do you agree with Loyola's cure for times of despair or desolation: to stand firm and hold to our prior convictions? Why or why not?

Philip expounds on Loyola's words: "Obedience, and only obedience, offers a way out." In times of darkness and despair, obedience is more difficult than ever because our emotions are screaming for a way out of our distress. Obedience seems to offer no out. It may also feel inauthentic. Why should a person do what is completely against his or her inclinations in a period of crisis? Is this advice psychologically unhealthy?

How does Proverbs 3:1–8 speak to these questions?

3. Andrew Greeley said, "If one wishes to eliminate uncertainty, tension, confusion and disorder from one's life, there is no point in getting mixed up either with Yahweh or with Jesus of Nazareth" (p. 92). How does this view square with your view of Christianity? Do you think churches oversell how the Christian life will work out? How can Christians promise unbelievers peace and rest through a relationship with Christ yet affirm Greeley's statement as well?

Philip writes, "I used to believe that Christianity solved problems and made life easier. Increasingly, I believe that my faith complicates life, in ways it should be complicated. As a Christian, I cannot *not* care about the environment, about homelessness and poverty, about racism and religious persecution, about injustice and violence. God does not give me that option" (p. 93). Does God really mean for us to be distressed about these sorts of issues? Doesn't faith mean that we trust God to take care of these problems and spend our energy on loving him? (See also the paragraphs on Elton Trueblood on page 94.)

4. Review Alvin Plantinga's philosophical argument about the faith involved in knowing both other people and God (p. 103). Have you ever been surprised to learn how much you didn't know about a person you thought you knew well? When have you been frustrated in knowing that someone close to you did not in fact know the real you?

   If we are limited in the degree to which we can really know one another, how much can we expect to truly know God? Should this knowledge discourage us in our relationship with God, or should it help us to accept the limitations we feel in knowing him, while also exciting us about the depths of God we have yet to discover?

5. Philip says, "I conceive of the spiritual life as a capacity built into the human person, but one that can only develop in relationship with God." Are you more in tune with spiritual things now than you were before you were in relationship with God? Do you see and feel things from a spiritual perspective in a way you did not before? If you answered yes, why do you think this is so?

6. Philip compares a relationship with God to a marriage relationship. "Early in our marriage," he writes, "an older and wiser couple counseled, 'Don't depend on romantic love. It won't last. Love is a decision, not a feeling.' . . . Yes, marriage lives on love, but it is the kind of love that parenthood demands, or Christian discipleship: a gritty decision to go forward, step by step, one foot in front of the other" (pp. 111–12).

If you are married, have you found the older couple's advice to be true? Are there times when spouses must love in the absence of affection? Do you approach your relationship with God the same way? Why or why not? If you are not married, do you find a comment like this disillusioning? Does it burst the romantic bubble?

Do you have any prayer needs to share with the group?

GRASPING FOR UNDERSTANDING OF MYSELF, MY GOD (10–20 MINUTES OR MORE)

We can talk about and even agree on the need for a daily, disciplined walk of faith regardless of our feelings or the doubts that persist. Yet just as necessary as a disciplined worship of God is a true image of the God we are worshiping. Today let's examine our personal image of God and then hold this image up to the true picture God paints of himself in the Bible. Depending on the time available, you may choose to reflect on these questions either now with your group or at home during personal time.

- What were your parents like when you were growing up? Were they ever stern, emotionally distant, too lenient, unpredictable, self-righteous, belittling, angry, troubled, addicted, depressed, driven, demanding, busy, judgmental, down on themselves?
- How closely does your image of God resemble your parents, either positive or negative?

- What image of God did you receive from the church or religious community in which you grew up?
- How much has this image of God stayed with you into adulthood?
- What is the most dominant characteristic of God in the image you hold of him? Is this part of your image an accurate one?
- Is there a void in your image of God because you have rejected prior images presented to you but have not come to a true sense of who God is?
- How much is your personal image of God affecting the depth of relationship you have with God?

If you feel your image of God, although ingrained, is inaccurate and is preventing you from developing a life-giving intimacy with him, spend some time looking at what God tells you about himself. Pray that God will begin a work of healing in you, transforming your view of him into a true picture of himself. Turn often to the following verses.

God's holiness: Leviticus 10:3; 1 Samuel 2:2; Psalm 77:13; Isaiah 5:16; 40:25; John 6:69; 1 Peter 1:15

God's faithfulness: Numbers 23:19; Deuteronomy 4:31; 7:9; 1 Samuel 15:29; Psalm 9:10; Isaiah 54:10; 2 Timothy 2:13; Hebrews 10:23; 2 Peter 3:9

God's love: Psalm 23:6; 146:8; Jeremiah 31:3; 32:41; Hosea 14:4; Zephaniah 3:17; Matthew 6:26; John 3:16; 16:27; Romans 8:32; Ephesians 2:4–7; 2 Thessalonians 2:16–17; 1 John 4:10, 16, 19

God's forgiveness: Psalm 103:10–11; Matthew 6:14; 11:25; Acts 13:39; 1 Corinthians 6:11; Colossians 1:21–22; 1 John 1:9

God's protection and help: Deuteronomy 33:12; Psalm 4:8; 22:24; 32:7; 46:1; Proverbs 18:10; Isaiah 43:2

God's comfort: Psalm 27:14; 55:22; John 16:33; 2 Corinthians 1:5

God's guidance: Psalm 32:8; 48:14; 73:23–24; Proverbs 3:6; 16:9; Isaiah 28:6; 30:1

CLINGING TO GOD DESPITE THE DISTANCE
(5 – 10 MINUTES)

Now we will take a few minutes to be silent together before God. Pray that God would help you to live a daily faith despite your doubts or lack of feeling toward him. Or pray that God would bring transformation to your image of him, helping you to know him as he truly is, good and powerful and loving. Use either of the following verses to help center your prayer.

> Be imitators of God, therefore, as dearly loved children and live a life of love, just as Christ loved us and gave himself up for us as a fragrant offering and sacrifice to God.
>
> EPHESIANS 5:1–2

> My purpose is that they may be encouraged in heart and united in love, so that they may have the full riches of complete understanding, in order that they may know the mystery of God, namely, Christ, in whom are hidden all the treasures of wisdom and knowledge.
>
> COLOSSIANS 2:2–3

LONGING FOR GOD IN THE WEEK AHEAD (OPTIONAL)

You can integrate this study into your life throughout the week by using the following suggestions and readings.

- Each morning, center your thoughts and prayers on living today in love for God and others.
- Be especially conscious of your thoughts about God. When you begin to envision God with an untrue characteristic, pray, "God, help me to know you as you truly are."
- In the week ahead as your time allows, reflect on the Bible passages listed previously in the section "Grasping for Understanding of Myself, My God," using the following schedule.

  Day 1: God's holiness and faithfulness
  Day 2: God's love
  Day 3: God's forgiveness
  Day 4: God's protection, help, and comfort
  Day 5: God's guidance

The following reading is excerpted and adapted from the book *Your God Is Too Small* by J. B. Phillips.

> Of course we are not entirely at the mercy of our own reluctance to commit ourselves! We want to satisfy our cravings for reality, we want to know the meaning of life and to have spiritual fundamentals upon which we may build a faith to live by. We want,

in short, to know God. Jesus Christ gave three remarkable indications by which men could *know* (not by scientific "proof," but by an inward conviction that is perfectly valid to him in whom it arises) that His claim and His revelation are true. They are contained in three sayings of His which are all well known:

(a) If any man will do his (i.e. God's) will, he shall know of the doctrine, whether it be of God or whether I speak of myself (John 7:17). Sometimes acting must come before knowing.
(b) He that hath seen me hath seen the Father (John 14:9). If you want to know what God is like, look at Jesus.
(c) I am the way, the truth, and the life: no man cometh unto the Father, but by me (John 14:6). Only Jesus can lead you truly to God the Father.

These three sayings, especially the last two, are intolerably arrogant if they come from a purely human moral teacher. Let us consider their significance [we will look only at the first in this excerpt]:

(a) Jesus says, in effect, that there will be no inward endorsement of the truth of the way of living he puts forward as the right one until a man is prepared to do the will, i.e. co-operate with the purpose, of God. This at once rules out arm-chair critics of Christianity and any dilettante appraisals of its merits. "You can't know," says Christ, "until you are willing to do."

It is plain from the Gospels that Christ regarded the self-loving, self-regarding, self-seeking spirit as the direct antithesis of real living. His two fundamental rules for life were that the "love-energy," instead of being turned in on itself, should go out first to God and then to other people. "If any man will come after me," he said, "let him deny himself (i.e. deny his tendency to love himself) and take up his cross (i.e. bear the painful cost of that denial) and follow me (i.e. live positively according to the principles that I teach and demonstrate)." Now the moment a man does this, even temporarily and tentatively, he finds himself in touch with something more real than he has known before. There is a sense that he is touching a deep and powerful stream that runs right through life. In other words, the moment he begins really to love, he finds himself in touch with the life of God.[1]

C H A P T E R S 9 – 1 0

UNDERSTANDING GOD THE FATHER

—— ✺ ——

The excerpt below is from *Reaching for the Invisible God*.

In the Bible life with God reads more like a mystery story, or a romance, than a theology text. What I find in its pages differs markedly from what I expect, and what most people expect, in getting to know God. The following aspects of God's personality may surprise and perplex someone seeking a personal relationship.

God is shy. By that, I do not mean bashful or timid, like a junior high boy at a party. Rather, God is shy to intervene. Considering the many things that must displease him on this planet, God exercises incredible— at times maddening—self-restraint.

Why this quality? I cannot speak for God, of course, but the answer must in part reflect the "problem" of an invisible Being relating to people in a material world. Unlike us, God has an all-encompassing point of view that takes in the world we see as well as other realms hidden to us. Moreover, God sees all our history at once, as a ball of yarn compared to the short, consecutive scraps of thread we experience. Unconstrained by a body, God exists in every place at once. Every time God chooses to manifest himself in our world, he must accept limitations. He "con-descends" (literally, descends to be with) to our point of view.

—— ✺ ——

God hides. According to the Jewish philosopher Martin Buber, "The Bible knows of God's hiding His face, of times when the contact between Heaven and earth seems to be interrupted. God seems to with-draw Himself utterly from the earth and no longer to participate in its existence. The space of history is then full of noise, but as it were, empty of divine breath." Do we live in such a time now, I sometimes wonder: full of noise but empty of God? And why would God flash his presence brightly one moment and not the next, like a firefly too quick to catch?

If God merely wanted to make his existence known to every person on earth, God would not hide. However, the direct presence of God would inevitably overwhelm our freedom, with sight replacing faith. God wants instead a different kind of knowledge, a personal knowledge that requires a commitment from the one who seeks to know him.

———— ⟶ ————

God is gentle. I know no better way to convey this truth than by contrast. Mark 9 gives a vivid description of possession by an evil spirit. Contrast that scene with possession by the Holy Spirit. "Quench not the Spirit," Paul warns in one place; "grieve not the holy Spirit of God," he says in another. God humbles himself so deeply that he puts himself somehow at our mercy. Whereas an evil spirit throws a person into fire or water, cre-ating a grotesque caricature of a human being, a sovereign God takes up residence in that same person and says, "Don't hurt me." You can only grieve, or hurt, someone who has emotions, who cares deeply.

I see the same gentleness and refusal to coerce in the life of God's Son. In dealing with people, he states the consequences of a choice, then hands the decision back to the other party. Jesus showed a fathomless respect for human freedom: even as people killed him he prayed, "Father, forgive them, for they do not know what they are doing."

———— ⟶ ————

God's presence varies. "How faint the whisper we hear of him," said Job during the long period of God's silence. By the end of the book, he could have amended that to "How loud the roar we hear of him!" Within the pages of one book the same person experiences an over-whelming sense of God's presence and also God's absence.

I have learned one absolute principle in calculating God's presence or absence, and that is that I cannot. God, invisible, sovereign, who accord-ing to the psalmist "does whatever pleases him," sets the terms of the relationship. As the theologian Karl Barth insisted so fiercely, God is *free:*

free to reveal himself or conceal himself, to intervene or not intervene, to work within nature or outside it, to rule over the world or even to be despised and rejected by the world, to display himself or limit himself. Our own human freedom derives from a God who cherishes freedom.

I cannot control such a God. At best I can put myself in the proper frame to meet him. I can confess sin, remove hindrances, purify my life, wait expectantly, and—perhaps hardest of all—seek solitude and silence. I offer no guaranteed method to obtain God's presence, for God alone governs that. Solitude and silence merely supply the state most conducive to attending to the still, small voice of God.

My choice of words may seem irreverent, but I intend to look at the Trinity in light of the "advantages" and "disadvantages" each person brings to the process of knowing God. No human being could possibly grasp the full Essence of God. We know the invisible God only as God reveals himself to us, in various Expressions. And whenever the invisible God con-descends in a way that we can perceive in our material world, we benefit in certain ways and suffer in others.

We identify physical objects by their qualities, but we get to know people mainly through their stories. In a similar way, we know God the Father primarily through stories from the Old Testament. God has the capacity to relate to all creation at once, upholding its existence, as the Hebrews celebrated in their psalms of nature and thanksgiving. Yet God also chose to relate on a closer level with a tribe of people descended from Abraham, Isaac, and Jacob. So closely did God get involved, in fact, that he "moved in" with them, first in a tent in the wilderness, later in a temple built by Solomon. They needed his actual presence in order to get to know him. Most important, God established a "covenant" with Israel, a contract that set the terms for both parties.

In addition, God made rare but dramatic appearances to individuals. God, who relates to the physical world at all points, decided to impinge upon it in one particular point, to choose a body or bush or dream as a vehicle of his presence. God could be seen and heard by humans through their physical sensors of eyes and ears. In the cloud and pillar of fire in the Sinai wilderness, the display continued for some time.

REACHING FOR THE INVISIBLE GOD STUDY GUIDE

My book *Disappointment with God* explored three questions many Christians ask: Is God hidden? Is God silent? Is God unfair? It struck me with great force as I wrote the book that those questions did not trouble the Hebrews in the Sinai wilderness. They saw evidence of God every day, heard him speak, and consorted under terms of a fair contract signed in God's own hand. Out of this relationship emerged the Jews' great gift to the world: monotheism, the belief in one sovereign, holy God.

Modern Americans, who tend to treat God more like a cosmic Good Buddy, could use a refresher course from the Old Testament on God's majesty. Pastor and author Gordon MacDonald has said that his own love for God has moved away from a sentimental model, which never satisfied, to something closer to a father/son model. He is learning to reverence, obey, and thank God; to express appropriate sorrow for blunders and sin; to pursue a quietness in which he might hear God whisper. In other words, he is seeking a relationship with God appropriate to the profound difference between the two parties.

———— ∾ ————

What "disadvantages" to knowing God might the Old Testament present? Love tends to decrease as power increases, and vice versa. The same power that repeatedly overwhelmed the Israelites made it difficult for them to perceive God's love.

I have concluded that most Christians today avoid the Old Testament for the simple reason that they find the God depicted there scary and remote. In Doris Lessing's wry phrase, "Jehovah does not think or behave like a social worker." Jehovah behaves, instead, like a holy God trying desperately to communicate to cantankerous human beings. In my own reading of the Old Testament, I used to look for ways to make God more acceptable, less fierce. Now I concentrate on making myself more acceptable to God, which was the point of the Old Testament, after all. God sought intimacy with his people, surely, albeit only on his terms.

Listen to God's own verdict on Old Testament times: "But my people would not listen to me; Israel would not submit to me. So I gave them over to their stubborn hearts to follow their own devices."

Israel's experience shows that God can be driven away or forced into hiding as a result of what people do. Sometimes God allows *us* to determine the intensity of his presence.

ENCOUNTERING GOD THROUGH THOSE IN THE BIBLE (10 MINUTES)

Today, in dramatic reading form, we will focus on three Scripture passages, about God, Jesus, and the Holy Spirit. Stay together as a large group for this reading time. Choose five volunteers who enjoy reading dramatically, and present the following readings to the class. Follow the gender assignments only as you are able.

Reading 1

Reader 1 (male): Read the two middle paragraphs on page 133 in the book, beginning with the words "One scene . . . "
Reader 2 (female): Read 1 Kings 19:5–12.

Reading 2

Reader (male): Read John 8:2–11.

Reading 3

Reader 1 (male): Read John 14:26; 16:7, 13–15.
Reader 2 (female): Read slowly and meditatively Galatians 5:22–23.

REACHING FOR GOD WITH OTHERS (20 MINUTES)

If you are in a large group, break into groups of four to six for this discussion time. Introduce yourselves to each other if necessary. Briefly discuss together: Have you ever taken a personality test of any sort, such as the kind that suggests whether you are an introvert or extrovert, etc.? If so, did you agree with the results?

1. If a well-known Christian psychologist were to announce that he had given God a personality test and the results showed a distinct quality of shyness in God, in the form of hesitancy to act, would you agree with the results? In looking at your life so far, can you see more instances in which God refrained from acting, or more times when it was fairly clear to you that he did act? When you look at the circumstances in our nation and in our world during your lifetime, has God been more prone to act or not act? How about in our world since the time of Christ?

Consider the story we just read of Elijah in 1 Kings. Why would God make such a powerful statement about himself through the fire on the wet altar and then allow wicked rulers like Ahab and Jezebel to continue their ungodly reign?

Why would Elijah, so soon after witnessing God's miraculous demonstration, flee in desperation and distrust? Why, in response, would God choose to interact with Elijah in a different way, through a quiet, personal, unimpressive voice? (See the last paragraph on page 131.)

Have you ever, like Elijah, become desperate and distrustful, or perhaps just lonely and depressed, in spite of seeing God act clearly on your behalf? Why do we so soon forget that God is in control?

Has God ever used a "whisper" to speak to you? How well did you hear him?

2. What about Philip's suggestion that God has a habit of hiding from people? Would you concur? In your experience has God seemed hard to find?

Review the stories of hide-and-seek told by Belden C. Lane on pages 116–17. Consider the statement "God is like a person who clears his throat while hiding and so gives himself away." And "God is for me a seven-year-old daughter, slipping back across the grass, holding her breath in check, wanting once again to surprise me with a presence closer than I could ever have expected." Can you think of one time in your life when God has acted in these ways with you? Share as much as you are comfortable with the group.

How has God, through both his hiddenness and his unmistakable presence, encouraged your growth in faith?

3. Does God exhibit a quality of gentleness, a refusal to coerce? Would you find this pattern to be true in your life? Has God allowed you to make your own decisions and lead your own life if you have so chosen? Have you appreciated this quality in God, or have you had times in which you'd rather God was sitting across the table telling you what to do?

How does the passage about Jesus in John 8 speak to his gentleness? In what ways could Jesus have coerced the Pharisees? Might he have made public their specific sins? How could he have coerced the woman? Might he have asked whether she was repentant?

Philip says, "God recognizes that *we* are the ones on the journey, not himself. The journey does not transpire like a treasure hunt, such that if we follow the instructions and look hard enough we will find the treasure. No, the journey itself is the goal. The very quest for God, our determined pursuit, changes us in the ways that matter most" (p. 120). When has your life with God seemed more like a frustrating treasure hunt than a meaningful journey? Have you ever felt that if you could only discover God's specific will for you in an area, then your life would begin to run smoothly? Or have you felt that if you could discover God's answer to some questions about living, then certain problems would be resolved? What exactly were you hunting for? Did you find it? What did you learn about your hunt? About God? About life with God?

4. Philip writes that God's presence in our lives is sometimes unmistakable and sometimes seemingly nonexistent. We can't control our sense of his presence. We can put ourselves into a proper frame to meet him, practicing regular periods of solitude and silence. Review the quote by C. S. Lewis on pages 121–22. Do you by nature follow the slogan "The best never rest"? Are you comfortable being alone and quiet? When alone, do you automatically turn on a stereo, television, or computer? Have you had the experience of your conscience, or God, speaking to you during a quiet moment? Why do many of us tend to avoid periods of silence? What is it about disengaging our minds and quieting our surroundings that provides an opportunity for God to speak?

5. When have you created something? Think about the process you went through in creating. Can you identify your stages of Idea, Expression, and Recognition, as Philip discusses on pages 124–25?

UNDERSTANDING GOD THE FATHER

Is it difficult for you to think about God as one Being expressed in three persons? Which part of God in the Trinity is most difficult for you to understand or develop a relationship with: God the Father, Jesus the Son, or the Holy Spirit? Modify or expound on the options below.

- God the Father. I can't get rid of the image of God as a mean old tyrant who is just waiting to jump on me for doing something wrong. This image affects my whole Christian life.
- Jesus the Son. I've had some very difficult experiences with men in my life, and because Jesus was a man who walked the earth, I am uncomfortable and afraid of him. I know he loved the children and healed the sick, but because he had authority, I can't shake my fear of him. Or, Jesus as a perfect human being makes me nervous. Relating to a spirit feels easier than relating to a God who was a man like me yet was so different from me.
- The Holy Spirit. I've heard or witnessed some pretty wild things involving the Holy Spirit. That stuff repels me. If the Holy Spirit initiates strange behavior and extreme encounters with God, I don't want a strong connection with the Spirit.

Can you think of a time when you sensed God guiding and counseling you through the Holy Spirit, as John 14 and 16 discuss? If you are a believer, consider the words of Galatians 5:22–23 as read earlier. Have you seen the fruits of the Spirit become more evident in your life during your time as a Christian? How so? If you are not a believer, do you know Christians whose lives are filled with these qualities?

6. Philip writes, "Modern Americans, who tend to treat God more like a cosmic Good Buddy, could use a refresher course from the Old Testament on God's majesty." Read the rest of his words about Gordon MacDonald at the top of page 130. Would you say that you tend

to view God as more of a Good Buddy or as one deserving of many approaches, including reverence, obedience, thanks, repentance, and quiet attentiveness?

Why, as MacDonald says, does a sentimental model of God (God seen only as friend/lover) fail to satisfy us? How and why does a sentimental model set us up for frustration and criticism of God? Can you relate personally to the process he describes?

7. Read the middle paragraph on page 132, beginning with "I have concluded ..." Consider Lessing's words "God does not behave like a social worker." Do you allow God to act "outside the box" of social worker in your life? Do you let him discipline you, give straightforward commands, direct you to make non-status-quo choices for your life?

Reflect on your approach to communicating God to your neighbors, your children, your coworkers. Do you tend to convey God as a holy social worker, one who is peaceable and careful not to offend? If so, why do you convey God this way? How can we communicate truthfully about God's holiness and sovereignty without being unloving and self-righteous?

Philip says, "I used to look for ways to make God more acceptable, less fierce. Now I concentrate on making myself more acceptable to God, which was the point of the Old Testament, after all"

(p. 132). As in all relationships, a satisfying connection with God is much more likely if we focus on being the right person rather than on making the other person right for us. Does this concept help you to feel more at peace with an Old Testament God who has troubled you, or does it make you feel angry or anxious at having the onus placed on you?

Do you have any prayer needs to share with the group?

GRASPING FOR UNDERSTANDING OF MYSELF, MY GOD (10–20 MINUTES OR MORE)

Just as we have looked in depth at God's personality today, it will be helpful now for us to look at pieces of our own personality. We have discussed the need for being the right people for God rather than continually expecting God to be what we deem the right God for us. Some parts of our personality will make this more difficult to do than others. Consider the following questions and, as time permits, discuss them with your small group or spend personal time reflecting on them.

- Do you tend to be more of a flexible team-player or a person who likes to make the decisions and direct others?
- Do you tend to be very passionate about what you feel to be the right way of going about things, or are you content to do what seems necessary at the time?
- Are you relatively comfortable with the place of mystery and uncertainty in your life, or are you driven to possess as much understanding as possible?
- Are you more of a thinker or a feeler, more intellectually or emotionally driven?
- Do you have some of the artist in you? Do you look more deeply into life and truth than does the rest of the population?

Underline the above personality traits that best describe you. Certainly, none of the traits dictate a person's perspective in relating to God. Yet we naturally respond out of our inner core: For instance, an in-charge, decision-maker personality might have a hard time letting God call the shots. Or this personality might understand better than anyone the need for allowing God to be the ultimate decision-maker. Our maturity as well as our perspective will influence how the various facets of our personality affect our relationship with God.

Review the underlined descriptions of yourself. Does each characteristic work in your life to make you more prone or less prone to be for God rather than expect of him? Can you think of ways in which you could make your personality traits work for you rather than against you—that is, push you toward living according to God's standard rather than toward demanding that God live according to yours?

CLINGING TO GOD DESPITE THE DISTANCE
(5 – 10 MINUTES)

Now we will take a few minutes to be silent together before God. This exercise can have a vital impact on positioning us in the necessary heart posture before God—the position in which God can begin to do soul-filling, extraordinary work in our lives. If as a group you feel fairly free with one another (or perhaps even if you do not), get out of your chairs and kneel on the floor. Enter a posture of prayer, kneeling upright with your arms extended up and out or bending your body to the floor and extending your arms before you. Tell God silently that you are giving yourself to him to be made into the person he created you to be. Thank him for being God, for being good, for doing as he, in his holiness, chooses to do. Ask God to further develop this attitude of release in your life.

If your group is not emotionally comfortable or able to kneel as described, envision yourself in this posture as you pray. Either way, accept the tears that may come. Surrendering to God is an emotional act. God welcomes your tears and counts them as an offering to him.

LONGING FOR GOD IN THE WEEK AHEAD
(OPTIONAL)

You can integrate this study into your life throughout the week by reflecting on the following Bible passages and the reading.

Day 1: Genesis 6:5–7:12
Day 2: Exodus 3:1–14
Day 3: Job 1:6–22
Day 4: Ecclesiastes 1:1–18
Day 5: Isaiah 57:14–19

The following reading is taken from *Revelations of Divine Love: The Seventh Revelation* by Julian of Norwich. Julian lived in the fourteenth century as a Benedictine nun in Norwich, England. With *Revelations of Divine Love* she became the first great female writer of the English language. Her theology is based on her mystical experiences. Julian experienced a serious illness at the age of thirty, yet despite her varying sense of God's presence, she held to the goodness and love of God. She is known for her words "All shall be well and all shall be well, and all manner of things shall be well."

Julian's writing and language are clearly from an earlier period, but if we work at reading and understanding her words, we can gain a great deal of encouragement and solidarity. The human soul has undergone struggles similar to hers for centuries. How grateful we can be that God's love as well endures.

And after this He shewed a sovereign ghostly pleasance in my soul. I was fulfilled with the everlasting sureness, mightily sustained without any painful dread. This feeling was so glad and so ghostly that I was in all peace and in rest, that there was nothing in earth that should have grieved me.

This lasted but a while, and I was turned and left to myself in heaviness, and weariness of my life, and irksomeness of myself, that scarcely I could have patience to live. There was no comfort nor no ease to me but faith, hope, and charity; and these I had in truth, but little in feeling.

And anon after this our blessed Lord gave me again the comfort and the rest in soul, in satisfying and sureness so blissful and so mighty that no dread, no sorrow, no pain bodily that might be suffered should have distressed me. And then the pain shewed again to my feeling, and then the joy and the pleasing, and now that one, and now that other, divers times—I suppose about twenty times. And in the time of joy I might have said with Saint Paul: *Nothing shall dispart me from the charity of Christ;* and in the pain I might have said with Peter: *Lord, save me: I perish!*

This Vision was shewed me, according to mine understanding, [for] it is speedful to some souls to feel on this wise: sometime to be in comfort, and sometime to fail and to be left to themselves. God willeth that we know that He keepeth us even alike secure in woe and in weal. And for profit of man's soul, a man is sometime left to himself; although sin is not always the cause: for in this time I sinned not wherefore I should be left to myself—for it was so sudden. Also I deserved not to have this blessed feeling. But freely our Lord giveth when He will; and suffereth us [to be] in woe sometime. And both is one love.

For it is God's will that we hold us in comfort with all our might: for bliss is lasting without end, and pain is passing and shall be brought to nought for them that shall be saved. And therefore it is not God's will that we follow the feelings of pain in sorrow and mourning for them, but that we suddenly pass over, and hold us in endless enjoyment.[1]

UNDERSTANDING JESUS AND THE HOLY SPIRIT

———— ᴄᴧᴖ ————

The excerpt below is from *Reaching for the Invisible God.*

Does God really want close contact with us? Jesus gave up heaven for it. In person he reestablished the original link between God and human beings, between seen and unseen worlds.

Jesus revealed a newly intimate side to God, a relationship so personal that he used the word "Abba," or "Daddy" to address him.* Jesus "came down from heaven," descending so far that in the process he made us more comprehensible to God. Not only do we understand God better because of Jesus; God understands *us* better.

My questions about providence and suffering are *primarily* answered in the person of Jesus, not in day-to-day events I may encounter now. I cannot learn from Jesus why bad things occur, but I can surely learn how God feels about such tragedies. Jesus gives God a face, and that face is streaked with tears.

In a fine analogy, H. Richard Niebuhr likened the revelation of God in Christ to the Rosetta stone. Before its discovery Egyptologists could only guess at the meaning of hieroglyphics. One unforgettable day they uncovered a dark stone that rendered the same text in Greek, ordinary Egyptian script, and previously indecipherable hieroglyphics. By comparing the translations side by side, they mastered hieroglyphics and could now see clearly into a world they had known only in a fog.

---

* To show the change in the emphasis: the Old Testament refers to God as Father 11 times, the New Testament 170 times.

———————

Niebuhr goes on to say that Jesus allows us to "reconstruct our faith." We can trust God because we trust Jesus. If we doubt God, or find him incomprehensible, unknowable, the very best cure is to gaze steadily at Jesus, the Rosetta stone of faith.

———— ❧ ————

In my spiritual journey as well as in my writing career I have long pondered unanswerable questions about the problem of pain, the conundrums of prayer, providence versus free will, and other such matters. When I do so, everything becomes fuzzy. Looking at Jesus, however, restores clarity.

As a major advantage in knowing God, then, Jesus offers a close-up portrait of God's own vantage point. What bothers me about this planet—injustice, poverty, racism, sexism, abuse of power, violence, disease—bothered him as well. By looking at Jesus, I gain insight into how God feels about what goes on down here. Jesus expresses the Essence of God in a way that we cannot misconstrue.

———— ❧ ————

One simple fact shows the "disadvantage" of Incarnation: few people acquainted with Jesus recognized his origin from God. For the duration of his time on earth, Jesus forfeited the privileges of God and thus risked going unrecognized. People expect power from their God, not powerlessness, strength not weakness, largeness not smallness.

Jesus orchestrated no lightning displays, and no cloud of smoke surrounded him when he addressed a crowd. By overcoming the disadvantages of the Old Testament revelations of God, Jesus lost the advantages. He looked not at all like God; he looked, well, human.

———— ❧ ————

Some Christians want to reproduce those times when God made himself more obvious. They regard the Spirit as a pet version of the Israelites' God in the wilderness: He speaks to them directly, provides food and clothing, guarantees health, offers crystal-clear guidance. In other words, the Spirit changes the rules of life so that we need never experience cause for disappointment. I know too many sick and needy Christians to believe that.

I envision the Spirit not so much touching our mundane lives with a supernatural wand as bringing the Recognition (Dorothy Sayers' word) of God's presence into places we may have overlooked. The Spirit may bring that jolt of Recognition to the most ordinary things: a baby's grin, snow falling on a frozen lake, a field of lavender in morning dew, a worship ritual that unexpectedly becomes more than ritual. Suddenly we see these momentary pleasures as gifts from a God who is worthy of praise.

Nevertheless, no one who wants to know God can ignore the Spirit, who made a dramatic appearance on earth at a hinge moment. As Jesus said goodbye to his followers, he asked them first to do something very important: Wait, Jesus said. Return to Jerusalem and wait for the Holy Spirit.

What has happened since Jesus' departure challenges faith and, in all honesty, drives many people away from God. In Jesus, God had deliberately joined a world infected with evil and fallen victim to it. With the Spirit, a holy God risked his reputation on the evil-infected persons themselves, by expanding the Incarnation to encompass all of Jesus' followers. The God who took on human flesh so that we could experience him in our material world still takes on human flesh—our flesh.

Yet read the sad, speckled history of the church. To put it mildly, mortal human beings do not embody God's Expression as well as Jesus did. What "advantages" are there to this final revelation of God?

We receive "gifts of the Spirit" from One who, by living inside us, knows precisely how each person's unique combination of personality, upbringing, and natural skills can be used in God's service. The Spirit enhances and shapes but never overwhelms our individual personalities and talents.

The Spirit announces the good news that we need not figure out exactly how to pray. We need only groan. Linking the *groans* of Romans 8, Paul tells of a Spirit who lives inside us, who detects needs we cannot articulate and expresses them in a language we cannot comprehend. When we don't know what to pray, the Spirit fills in the blanks.

The Bible presents, if you will, a "trinity of groans," a progression of intimacy in God's involvement with his creation. The Old Testament tells us of a God above, a Father who attends to our dwarfish human needs. The Gospels tell of a further step, the God alongside, who became one of us, taking on ears, vocal cords, and pain cells. And the Epistles tell of the God within, an invisible Spirit who gives expression to our wordless needs. The "groaning" chapter of Romans 8 concludes with the bold promise that one day there will be no need for groans at all.

The "disadvantage" of knowing God through the Holy Spirit is that, when God turned over the mission to his church, he truly turned it over. As a result, many people who reject God are rejecting not God but a caricature of him presented by the church. Yes, the church has led the way in issues of justice, literacy, medicine, education, and civil rights. But to our everlasting shame, the watching world judges God by a church whose history also includes the Crusades, the Inquisition, anti-Semitism, suppression of women, and support of the slave trade.

I find it much easier to accept the fact of God dwelling in Jesus of Nazareth than in the people who attend my local church and in me. Yet the New Testament insists this pattern fulfills God's plan from the beginning: not a continuing series of spectacular interventions but a gradual delegation of his mission to flawed human beings. All along, Jesus planned to die so that we, his church, could take his place. What Jesus brought to a few—healing, grace, hope, the good-news message of God's love—his followers could now bring to all.

God's withdrawal behind human skin, his condescension to live inside common people, guarantees that all will sometimes doubt and many will reject God altogether. The plan also guarantees that the kingdom will advance at a slow, tedious pace, which God, showing remarkable restraint, does not overrule.

We all want a divine problem-solver. Christians may feel the same impatience over the slow, unspectacular work of the Holy Spirit as Jews felt over Jesus the Messiah, who did not provide the kind of triumphant rescue they wanted. The questions we ask of God, he often turns back on us. We plead for God to "come down" and only reluctantly acknowledge that God is already here, within us, and that what God does on earth closely resembles what the church does. In short, the chief "disadvantage" to knowing God as Spirit is the history of the church—and the spiritual biography of you and me.

ENCOUNTERING GOD THROUGH THOSE IN THE BIBLE (10 MINUTES)

Again this week we will present a dramatic reading of Scripture. Choose three volunteers to read slowly and reflectively: a narrator, a disciple, and

Jesus. Readers should refrain from reading Scripture references in brackets. Stay together as a large group for this reading time.

———— ⬥ ————

NARRATOR: Step back for a moment and contemplate God's point of view. A Spirit unbound by time and space, God had borrowed material objects now and then—a burning bush, a pillar of fire—to make himself obvious on planet Earth. Each time, God adopted the object in order to convey a message, as an actor might don a mask, and then moved on.

In Jesus something new happened: God *became* one of the planet's creatures, an event unparalleled, unheard of, unique in the fullest sense of the word. The God who fills the universe imploded to become a peasant baby who, like every infant who has ever lived, had to learn to walk and talk and dress himself. In the Incarnation, God's Son deliberately "handicapped" himself, exchanging omniscience for a brain that learned Aramaic phoneme [foe-neem] by phoneme, omnipresence for two legs and an occasional donkey, omnipotence for arms strong enough to saw wood but too weak for self-defense. God's perfect Expression was, scandalously, not what anyone could have come up with on their own.

As he prepared to leave, Jesus promised the Holy Spirit, a Comforter who would achieve an intimacy so close that we somehow participate in the very actions of God on earth. "God is spirit," insisted Jesus. But how to imagine a Spirit or visualize God apart from some visible form? We humans search for clear-cut signs of God's presence, as if still yearning for the burning bush or audible voice. Can we ever determine whether a Spirit-God is interacting with life on this planet? In short, how can we believe in a God we cannot see?

DISCIPLE: Lord, show us the Father and that will be enough for us [John 14:8].

JESUS: Don't you know me? [John 14:9].

NARRATOR: Although he was a son, he learned obedience from what he suffered and, once made perfect, he became the source of eternal salvation [Hebrews 5:8–9].

DISCIPLE: Lord, show us the Father and that will be enough for us.

JESUS: Don't you know me?

NARRATOR: Who, being in very nature God, did not consider equality with God something to be grasped, but made himself nothing, taking the very nature of a servant, being made in human likeness. And being found in appearance as a man, he humbled himself and became obedient to death—even death on a cross! Therefore God exalted him to the highest place and gave him the name that is above every name, that at the name of Jesus every knee should bow, in heaven and on earth and under the earth, and every tongue confess that Jesus Christ is Lord, to the glory of God the Father [Philippians 2:6–11].

DISCIPLE: Lord, show us the Father and that will be enough for us.

JESUS: Don't you know me?

NARRATOR: Praise be to the God and Father of our Lord Jesus Christ, the Father of compassion and the God of all comfort, who comforts us in all our troubles [2 Corinthians 1:3–4].

DISCIPLE: Lord, show us the Father and that will be enough for us.

JESUS: Don't you know me?

NARRATOR: Jesus said, "I tell you the truth: It is for your good that I am going away. Unless I go away, the Counselor will not come to you; but if I go, I will send him to you" [John 16:7].

DISCIPLE: Lord, show us the Father and that will be enough for us.

JESUS: Don't you know me?

NARRATOR: The fruit of the Spirit is love, joy, peace, patience, kindness, goodness, faithfulness, gentleness and self-control [Galatians 5:22–23]. In the same way, the Spirit helps us in our weakness. We do not know what we ought to pray for, but the Spirit himself intercedes for us with groans that words cannot express [Romans 8:26].

DISCIPLE: Lord, show us the Father and that will be enough for us.

JESUS: Don't you know me?

NARRATOR: What, then, shall we say in response to this? If God is for us, who can be against us? He who did not spare his own Son, but gave him up for us all—how will he not also, along with him, graciously give us all things? ... Christ Jesus who died—more than that, who was raised to life—is at the right hand of God and is also interceding for us. Who shall separate us from the love of Christ? Shall trouble or hardship or persecution or famine or nakedness or danger or sword? ... No, in all these things we are more than conquerors though him who loved us. For I am convinced that neither death nor life, ... neither the present nor the future, nor any powers, ... will be able to separate us from the love of God that is in Christ Jesus our Lord [Romans 8:31–32, 34–35, 37–39].

DISCIPLE: Lord, show us the Father and that will be enough for us.

JESUS: Don't you know me?

NARRATOR: I saw heaven standing open and there before me was a white horse, whose rider is called Faithful and True. With justice he judges and makes war. His eyes are like blazing fire, and on his head are many crowns. He has a name written on him that no one knows but he himself. He is dressed in a robe dipped in blood, and his name is the Word of God. The armies of heaven were following him, riding on white horses and dressed in fine linen, white and clean. Out of his mouth comes a sharp sword with which to strike down the nations. "He will rule them with an iron scepter." He treads the winepress of the fury of the wrath of God Almighty. On his robe and on his thigh he has this name written: KING OF KINGS AND LORD OF LORDS [Revelation 19:11–16].

REACHING FOR GOD WITH OTHERS (20 MINUTES)

If you are in a large group, break into groups of four to six for this discussion time. Introduce yourselves to each other if necessary. Share with the others about one circumstance or role in your life that has played out differently than at one time you had imagined it would. Maybe your role as a single person or spouse, your career life, your situation as a parent, your financial status, your image of yourself at your current age.

1. What if Jesus walked the earth today? Would he be, in the words of pop singer Joan Osborne, "just a slob like one of us," a stranger on the bus commuting home? Do these words offend you? What idea about Jesus do these words help to accurately convey?

   Try to envision what someone might look like today who is the "everyman" of our society—not widely respected or noticed, not in a position to influence the society at large, simply a member of the daily grind. What would this person look like physically? What kind of job might he have? What would his financial situation be? What would his living accommodations be like? Where in your city would he live? Who would be his companions?

Why did the people of Jesus' day have difficulty believing that the man they saw before them was the Son of God? If Jesus walked the earth today, do you think you would be inclined to recognize him? Why or why not?

Envision the Jesus of today you described earlier (the "stranger on the bus"). Does an image of a God living day to day in this kind of situation seem like a God who could understand and come alongside your life? What is comforting about this kind of God?

2. Read the quote by Augustine in the footnote on page 136. As Augustine describes, every facet of Jesus' life as a human being represented the paradox of God becoming man, of God making himself accessible to us. In no other way could we have true intimacy with God. Have you considered the idea that in becoming man, God also "learned" a new intimacy with us, through sensing for the first time what it's like to be human and to suffer (top of page 138)? Does such a concept make you uncomfortable? Why would the Bible use a word like *learned* about the unchangeable God (Hebrews 5:8)? How does this idea make you feel about your questions on suffering and God's role in it?

Reread the paragraph about the discovery of the Rosetta stone at the top of page 139. In your own words, why is this analogy of the Rosetta stone useful in helping us understand Jesus' role in our faith?

UNDERSTANDING JESUS AND THE HOLY SPIRIT

How does Philip's analogy of Jesus as the magnifying glass of our faith help to put into perspective the unanswered questions in your life and faith? What specific questions about God do you struggle with that a focus on Jesus might help answer?

3. Review the story about French philosopher and anthropologist René Girard on pages 141–43. As Flannery O'Connor's character commented, "Jesus thrown everything off balance." How did Jesus' life and death on the cross set a foundation for solidarity between Christians and the politically correct activists of today? Why is it that activists such as women, the poor, minorities, the disabled, environmental and human-rights advocates often position themselves against Christians, when in fact the gospel first honored the victim? Are Christians sometimes responsible for the rift between themselves and activists? Why?

Philip writes, "In a culture that glorifies success and grows deaf to suffering, we need a constant reminder that at the center of the Christian faith hangs an unsuccessful, suffering Christ, dying in shame." Reflect quietly for a moment: How much in your life do you glorify success? How much attention do you give to others who are suffering? Is the magnifying glass of your life focused on what our culture exalts, the successful, or on what Jesus exalts, the weak? Share with the group: how can you shift your focus to make it more consistently in line with Jesus'?

4. Review the story of Roberta Bondi and her distorted image of God the Father on pages 143–44. How does her story help you look to

77

Jesus to help correct any distortions you might have in your image of God?

Is your image of Jesus distorted in any way? If so, what areas of Jesus' life do you need to focus on to help you see him as he really is? What areas do you need to focus on to help you understand how he feels about you?

5. In discussing Umberto Eco and his observation of Americans' material outlook on life, Philip writes, "As material beings, we devalue spirit as less real and want God to appear in the realm of matter, where we live." He adds, "Some Christians regard the Spirit as a pet version of the Israelites' God in the wilderness: He speaks to them directly, provides food and clothing, guarantees health, offers crystal-clear guidance. In other words, the Spirit changes the rules of life so that we need never experience cause for disappointment." What is your reaction to these words?

- Yancey's judgment is an immature, shallow view of the Holy Spirit. The Spirit is capable of all God is capable of. We can therefore expect the Spirit to provide in every way for us. The more we ask of the Holy Spirit, the more he will deliver.
- We should be very cautious to pooh-pooh other Christians' experiences of the Holy Spirit. God is still a miracle-working God, and as Scripture reminds, it is those with a childlike faith who most fully experience the kingdom of God.
- I agree that we cannot expect the Holy Spirit to grant our checklist of desires. But Jesus said, "[The Spirit] will bring glory to me by taking from what is mine and making it known to you. All that belongs to the Father is mine (John 16:14–15)." The Spirit is certainly able to do much more for us than many of us Christians ask him to do.

- I like the reminder that we Americans must think beyond the material world. Our culture is quick to enforce this one-dimensional perspective even in regard to faith. I want to experience the Holy Spirit in fullness and in truth, without an overemphasis on his provision of tangible things like money, health, or word-for-word guidance.

6. Consider the words of Galatians 5:22–23. Then identify a Christian in your life who embodies many of these fruits of the Spirit. Look at this person's life and then at your own. Are the gifts of the Spirit listed in Galatians manifested in a similar way in your lives, or do the gifts take on a distinctly different flavor in each case? Philip writes, "We receive 'gifts of the Spirit' from One who, by living inside us, knows precisely how each person's unique combination of personality, upbringing, and natural skills can be used in God's service" (p. 151). Can you share with the group about one way you believe God desires to use you because of your personality, upbringing, and natural skills?

7. Following John Taylor's analogy to Shakespeare's *Henry V,* Philip writes, "God's withdrawal behind human skin, his condescension to live inside common foot soldiers, guarantees that all will sometimes doubt and many will reject God altogether. The plan also guarantees that the kingdom will advance at a slow, tedious pace, which God, showing remarkable restraint, does not overrule. It took eighteen centuries for the church to rally against slavery, and even then many resisted. Poverty still abounds, as does war and discrimination, and in some places the church does little to help. . . . The questions we ask of God he often turns back on us. We plead for God to 'come down' and only reluctantly acknowledge that God is already here, within us, and that what God does on earth closely resembles what the church does."

Although God *allows* a slow, tedious pace in the working out of his kingdom through human beings, what kind of effort do you think he *desires* from us, his foot soldiers? Relaxed? Halfhearted? Passionate? Tireless?

Over what sorts of issues or needs are you most often distressed—humanitarian issues, moral issues, emotional suffering, health-related struggles, environmental issues, spiritual struggles? If "what God does on earth closely resembles what the church does," where do you need to be devoting more time, energy, money, or prayer?

Do you have any prayer needs to share with the group?

GRASPING FOR UNDERSTANDING OF MYSELF, MY GOD (10–20 MINUTES OR MORE)

Today we will examine in greater depth the role of the church and other Christians in our lives, in the past and the present. Then we will look at ourselves as a piece of the church and therefore of Christ, reaching out to the world.

First consider:

- What have been the two or three most difficult and pivotal trials of your life?
- During these trials, how, if at all, was a church community involved in your life? How were other Christians involved in helping throughout your trials?
- Did Christians offer emotional support? Material support? Spiritual support? Did they listen and empathize or merely preach? How could they have more effectively helped you?

- Do you feel that for the most part Christians contributed positively or negatively to your time of struggle? Did they act as Jesus to you?
- Are you now experiencing a significant struggle in which Christians are or are not offering Jesus' care?
- If you are part of a Christian community that seems unable to care for you as Jesus would, and no other Christians are available to help, begin to pray that Jesus would impart himself to you anyway, despite the seeming limitations.

Now consider:

- Do you still carry the deep wounds of being failed by a church or Christians in your time of need?
- Do you need to pray through a process of forgiving Christians for not being Jesus to you in your need?
- Do you focus more on how God, and to a great extent Christians, have failed you, or on how you can live out the presence of Christ in other needy lives?
- If your focus is more on the first than the second, what needs to happen to shift your focus?
- What might God be particularly asking you to do to represent Jesus to others?

Consider writing in a journal your reflections about the above questions. You may need to spend considerable time working through the questions and praying about them. You will find that the time spent will bring greater understanding of yourself, your pain, and the great potential Christians have for embodying Christ to others. Any group time you have to discuss the questions will also add helpful insights.

CLINGING TO GOD DESPITE THE DISTANCE
(5–10 MINUTES)

In a few minutes of silent prayer before God, choose to focus on one of the two options below.

1. If you were to name one prayer need for yourself or for someone else who has placed a burden on your heart recently, what would it be?

Hold this need in cupped hands before God as you pray the following verse to begin your prayer time.

The Spirit helps us in our weakness. We do not know what we ought to pray for, but the Spirit himself intercedes for us with groans that words cannot express.

ROMANS 8:26

After you pray this verse, continue holding the need in your hands before God. Focus on the need and on presenting it to God, but do not feel any words are necessary to accompany your prayer. Allow your prayer to be the placing of the need before God, and the trust that the Holy Spirit is groaning and interceding in a way that makes your prayer as effective as any worded prayer.

2. Ask God to transform your attitude toward him and his work in the world. Ask for his grace to make you a more effective Christ-carrier to a world that needs his healing. You may want to make one of the following prayers a part of your prayer.

Help me to spread your fragrance everywhere I go—let me preach you without preaching, not by words but by my example—by the catching force, the sympathetic influence of what I do, the evident fullness of the love my heart bears to you.

John Henry Newman

Lord, make me an instrument of your peace.
Where there is hatred, let me sow love,
Where there is injury, pardon,
Where there is doubt, faith,
Where there is despair, hope,
Where there is darkness, light,
Where there is sadness, joy.
O Divine Master, grant that I may not so much seek to be consoled
    as to console,
not so much to be understood as to understand,
not so much to be loved, as to love;
for it is in giving that we receive,
it is in pardoning that we are pardoned,
it is in dying, that we awake to eternal life.

FRANCIS OF ASSISI

LONGING FOR GOD IN THE WEEK AHEAD (OPTIONAL)

You can integrate this study into your life throughout the week by using the following readings.

Day 1: John 11:1–44
Day 2: John 12:1–8
Day 3: John 13:1–17
Day 4: John 14:15–31
Day 5: John 16:5–16

The following reflection by Brenda Quinn is excerpted from *Meet the Bible: A Panorama of God's Word in 366 Daily Readings and Reflections* by Philip Yancey and Brenda Quinn.

The book of Acts illustrates that life with the Holy Spirit adds another dimension to our faith. Our days can become unpredictably exciting, and our lives may take unexpected and miraculous turns. But life with the Spirit doesn't mean we become perfect. We will still fail and we will not always make the right decisions.

The apostles experienced drastic change, but they too did not become perfect. Ananias and Sapphira proved that people in Spirit-filled communities still go their own way sometimes. Living in the Spirit is a growth process of continually giving over control to him.

Hannah Whitall Smith, author of *The Christian's Secret of a Happy Life,* found this to be poignantly true. Catherine Marshall tells Smith's story [in her book *Something More* (Grand Rapids: Chosen, 1974), 276–81]. Born in Philadelphia in 1832 to a Quaker family, Smith felt from a young age a great zeal for spiritual things. Her Quaker upbringing gave her a thorough knowledge of the Bible, and she began to believe early on that Christians must know God primarily through what he says in his Word rather than through their emotions toward him. Emotions, she found, can be unreliable and deceptive.

Hannah and her husband, Robert, became part of a lively church and one summer attended a camp meeting at a woodland campsite. Here, in the woods, Robert had an emotional experience with the Holy Spirit. He felt the Spirit enter him in a way that brought joy and connection to God such as he'd never known.

Soon after, he became a powerful evangelistic teacher, drawing crowds wherever he spoke. Hannah, meanwhile, tried repeatedly to prompt a similar experience with the Holy Spirit, but to no avail. She realized in time that her experience with God was as real as her husband's but simply different. "She wanted emotions and was given conviction. She 'wanted a vision and got a fact.'"

Robert's success in preaching flourished but then was suddenly cut short. Gossip began circulating about improper conduct with females, causing him to lose the respect of audiences and the support of sponsors. We don't know how much truth the gossip contained, but it seems that at some level Robert let his emotions carry him to actions the Spirit wouldn't have prompted. He never regained his passion for living or sharing Christ. Hannah, meanwhile, kept on in a steady faith that strengthened her and enabled her to continue being used by God.

We learn from the Smith's story that if we let our emotions become our primary means of connection with God, we risk moving outside of the Spirit's control. We become prone to following our own urges. Marshall sees this emotionalism as a real danger for the church today. It can happen if we allow "too great a love affair with emotion, too little grounding in Scripture, too [much] wanting in garden-variety discipline, too small an emphasis on purity, strict honesty, morality—Christ's own life living in us. What is needed, of course, is a balance: plenty of solid teaching—but plenty of joy as well."

More, we need to have other believers in our life who can see when we're moving in a dangerous direction. "We must deliberately make ourselves subject one to the other," Marshall urges, "be willing to be checked and corrected as well as encouraged and strengthened."

We don't need to fear letting the Holy Spirit control our lives. He is God and we can fully trust him. When we continue to live in God's Word and walk each day in humility with him, we can trust the Spirit will protect us and lead us into a richer, more mature life with himself.[1]

INNER TRANSFORMATION

⎯⎯ ⌇ ⎯⎯

The excerpt below is from *Reaching for the Invisible God*.

Mark van Doren, the literature professor who once taught Thomas Merton, visited his former student at a Kentucky monastery after a thirteen-year separation. Van Doren and other friends of Merton still could not comprehend Merton's transformation from a New York party animal into a monk who cherished solitude and silence. Van Doren reported,

> Of course he looked a little older; but as we sat and talked I could see no important difference in him, and once I interrupted a reminiscence of his by laughing. "Tom," I said, "you haven't changed at all."
>
> "Why would I? Here," he said, "our duty is to be more ourselves, not less." It was a searching remark and I stood happily corrected.

I believe God has a similar goal for all of us, that we become more ourselves by realizing the "selves" God originally intended for us. A part of us now remains hidden and undeveloped, like an organ the function of which we've not yet ascertained. Yet the Spirit's work proceeds, invisibly and unendingly, to fashion our true selves. We cannot construct the personality that pleases God but God can and promises to do exactly that.

Toward the end of his life, Henri Nouwen said that prayer had become for him primarily a time of "listening to the blessing." "The real 'work' of prayer," he said, "is to become silent and listen to the voice that says good things about me." That may sound self-indulgent, he admitted, but not if it meant seeing himself as the Beloved, a person in whom God had chosen to dwell. The more he listened to that voice, the less likely he was to judge his worth by how others responded to him or by how much he achieved.

Rarely do I wake up in the morning full of faith. So often my faith, which seemed so certain the day before, disappears overnight and I wake up in a cloud of poisonous doubt.

I remind myself of what I deeply know: that my worth comes from God, who has lavished love and grace upon me. In relating to an invisible God, though, without a determined effort, my thoughts of him slip away. Distractions push aside God-consciousness. How can I keep from forgetting? How to cultivate the belief that God himself lives within me, even as I so regularly forget his presence?

Monastics have a practice they call *statio* that means, simply, stopping one thing before beginning another. Rather than rushing from one task to the next, pause for a moment and recognize the time between times. Do this often enough and even mechanical acts become conscious, mindful.

The visible world forces itself on me without invitation; I must consciously cultivate the invisible. I wish the process were spontaneous and natural, but I have never found it so. Indeed, I have found that such a process, like anything of worth, requires discipline. The Christian life involves daily acts of will, a deliberate reorientation to a new—and in some ways unnatural—personal identity.

I have often recalled the story of a man who came up to me after a speaking engagement and said, rather blusteringly, "You wrote a book titled *Where Is God When It Hurts,* didn't you?" When I nodded yes, he continued, "Well, I don't have time to read your book. Can you tell me what it says in just a sentence or two?"

I gave it some thought and replied, "Well, I suppose I'd have to answer with another question, 'Where is the church when it hurts?'" You see, I explained, the church is God's presence on earth, his Body.

And if the church does its job—if the church shows up at the scene of disasters, visits the sick, staffs the AIDS clinics, counsels the rape victims, feeds the hungry, houses the homeless—I don't think the world will ask that question with the same urgency. They will know where God is when it hurts: in the bodies of his people, ministering to a fallen world. Indeed, our consciousness of God's presence often comes as a byproduct of other people's presence.

———— ✺ ————

In the interest of full disclosure, I must confess that I have little personal experience of the more dramatic manifestations of God's presence. I have never spoken in tongues or barked in church, and not once have I been swept up in a public display of spiritual ecstasy. This may relate to awkward experiences from the past, to my fear of losing control, to spiritual inadequacy, or to a squelching streak of rationality. I do not know. What I do know, however, is that the New Testament writers consistently speak of the "spirit of Christ" and in fact use the phrases "in the Spirit" and "in Christ" almost interchangeably. Therefore, when I want to visualize God's Spirit—an oxymoron, I realize—I turn to Jesus, in whom the unseeable takes on a face.

Because of Jesus' life on earth, we have an actual and vivid representation of what a human being connected to God should look like. The "fruits of the Spirit" are in fact the qualities that Jesus showed on earth, and he promised to "abide," or make his home, in us to nurture those same qualities.

———— ✺ ————

Jesus never brainwashed anyone. To the contrary, he depicted the cost of following him in the most realistic terms imaginable ("Take up your cross and follow me"). He never imposed himself on another person but always left room for choice and even rejection. In that same style, any changes God works in a person will come about not as a result of coercion from the outside but by a Spirit working from within, summoning up new life, transforming from the inside out. The words used to describe God's Spirit—Comforter, Helper, Counselor—imply that change may involve a slow, internal process, with many fits and starts.

When I think of the fear and discomfort summoned up by mentioning the Holy Spirit, I have to laugh at the irony of being spooked by the

Comforter. Sometimes I secretly yearn for the spectacular—fits of ecstasy, miraculous answers to prayer, resurrections, healings—when the Holy Spirit chiefly offers a slow, steady progression toward the end God desires all along: the gradual reconstruction of my fallen self.

———— ⌒ ————

I have already mentioned the analogy of marriage, the most "adult" relationship that most people ever have. (Deep friendships show these same qualities as well.) In marriage two partners can achieve a unity while preserving their freedom and independence.

Even so, as every couple learns, combining two genders in a marriage introduces differences that may take a lifetime to work out. Joining a human being with God involves a whole new category of "incompatibilities." One partner is invisible, overwhelming, and perfect; the other is visible, weak, and flawed. How can the two possibly get along?

In some ways, the Holy Spirit acts as a kind of resident "marriage counselor" between myself and God. The analogy may seem far-fetched, but remember the New Testament's words to describe the Spirit: Comforter, Counselor, Helper. The Spirit comforts in moments of distress, calms me in times of confusion, and overcomes my fears. Consistently, the Bible presents the Spirit as the invisible inner force, the Go-Between God who assists us in relating to the transcendent Father.

Like every starry-eyed newlywed, Janet and I both learned that the wedding ceremony was just the beginning of the process of making love work. Our marriage has hardly been a place of serenity, void of negative emotions. To the contrary, we are more likely to express feelings of anger and disappointment to each other than to anyone else, even when "outside" forces prompt those feelings. A healthy marriage is not a problem-free place, but it can be a safe place. We know that we will still love each other the next day and the next, and that despite the strain, our love may well soothe the hurt that caused those feelings in the first place.

When I read the Psalms and Job and Jeremiah, I sense something of the same pattern at work. Notice the angry outbursts, the complaints, the wild accusations against God contained in those books. God offers a "safe place" to express ourselves, even the worst parts of ourselves. I heard little of that blunt honesty in church growing up, which I now see as a spiritual defect, not a strength. Christians, I have noticed, are not immune from the kinds of circumstances that provoked the outbursts in Job and Psalms. Why attempt to hide deep emotions from a God who dwells within, a Spirit who has promised to express on our behalf "groans" for which words fail us?

I will never be able to reduce life with God to a formula for the same reason I cannot reduce my marriage to a formula. It is a living, growing relationship with another free being, very different from me and yet sharing much in common. No relationship has proved more challenging than marriage. I am tempted sometimes to wish for an "old-fashioned" marriage, in which roles and expectations are more clearly spelled out and need not always be negotiated. I sometimes yearn for an intervention from outside which would decisively change one of the characteristics that bring my wife and me pain. So far, that has not happened. We wake up each day and continue the journey on ground that grows incrementally more solid with each step.

ENCOUNTERING GOD THROUGH THOSE IN THE BIBLE (5 MINUTES)

Today we will look at God's process of transforming us into the person he means us to be. Read the following Scripture passages in the order in which they appear. Pay special attention to the work and power of the Spirit expressed in these verses.

    Acts 9:1–22
    2 Timothy 1:6–7
    Psalm 139:1–24
    Ephesians 3:14–21

REACHING FOR GOD WITH OTHERS (25 MINUTES)

If you are in a large group, break into groups of four to six for this discussion time. Introduce yourselves to each other if necessary. Briefly discuss: If a comedian were to poke fun at the people of your geographical region of the country, what characteristics would he or she focus on?

1. Review Philip's discussion of his own "makeover" in high school on pages 161–62. Have you at some time in your life felt the need to change something about your identity? Maybe during adolescence

or young adulthood? Why did you feel the change was necessary? Was it successful?

Reread the paragraphs about Thomas Merton in the middle of page 163. Would you expect a "party animal transformed monk" to exhibit little noticeable outward change? Philip says, "I believe God has a similar goal for all of us, that we become more ourselves by realizing the 'selves' God originally intended for us." Does that idea give you a sense of relief or a sense of disappointment? Do you want to stay essentially who you are, or are you hoping for a more radical change?

Philip goes on to say, "It begins with trust in God's best for me, a confidence that God will liberate my true self, not bind it." Have you ever been afraid that God, if given free reign, will transform you into a monk or a missionary or a preacher or a skid row volunteer or some other role you see as undesirable? Are you more afraid of discovering God's best or discovering your true self? Do you believe the two are one and the same?

Philip writes, "The Spirit's work proceeds, invisibly and unendingly, to fashion our true selves. We cannot construct the personality that pleases God, but God can and promises to do exactly that" (p. 164). Look back at Psalm 139. What verses in this psalm speak of God's work in each of us proceeding invisibly and unendingly?

2. 1 John 3:20 speaks of those times when "our hearts condemn us," when we feel unacceptable to God. John reminds us that "God is greater than our hearts." His love is full of grace—existing because of who he is, not what we deserve. Love defines God's nature. Can you share about how God has helped you understand his grace in a fuller way so you are less condemning of yourself? Or do you still need work in believing God's love for you?

   Recall Henri Nouwen's words on prayer: "The real 'work' of prayer is to become silent and listen to the voice that says good things about me." One acronym for a suggested prayer format is ACTS: Adoration, Confession, Thanksgiving, Supplication. While this suggests a balanced way of speaking regularly to God, it encourages only that—speaking *to* God. Have you ever attempted to enter into prayer with the goal of listening rather than speaking? Why does Nouwen refer to this type of prayer as work? Why can this sort of prayer bring such a radical sense of freedom? How might a person incorporate listening prayer into his or her life on a regular basis?

   What does Ephesians 3:14–21 say about listening prayer? How does this passage support the idea of God being greater than our hearts?

3. Have you ever gone through an intense period of life in which your emotions peaked and ebbed on a daily basis? Have you ever felt this way about your spiritual life? Have you felt the Holy Spirit's presence in your spiritual swings, helping to anchor you? If so, how did you detect the Spirit's presence? Was it through more of a whisper in

the quiet or a loud demonstration amid the clatter? Did it take work to hear and respond to the Spirit? What kind of work?

What do you think of the practice of *statio,* performed by monks: the practice of stopping one thing before beginning another, pausing to reflect on what has just transpired or what is about to transpire (p. 168)? Is it an idea that sounds good but is not too practical? Is it something that over time could come somewhat naturally? Is your life right now conducive to such a practice? Why or why not?

Why would a practice like *statio* help a person avoid conforming to the world around us?

Philip says, "The visible world forces itself on me without invitation; I must consciously cultivate the invisible. I wish the process were spontaneous and natural, but I have never found it so. Indeed, I have found that such a process, like anything of worth, requires discipline. . . . The Christian life . . . involves daily acts of will, a deliberate reorientation to a new—and in some ways unnatural—personal identity" (p. 169). We began our discussion today with talk of God not so much changing us as bringing us into our true selves. Now Philip's words speak of self-discipline and work in the quest for a new and somewhat unnatural personality. How do these two ideas fit together? Consider the analogies of the musicians (p. 169). Does one who is, heart and soul, a pianist still need to practice? If so, does that mean that even when God brings me into my true self, I must still practice forms of spiritual discipline to stay in line with God and this true self? Does all cello playing serve only to improve the skill, or does some playing serve to improve the player? Does some discipline help me to continue discovering my true self, which sometimes feels contrary to my natural, human self?

4. Review the stories of the gospel choir and Martin Luther King Jr. on pages 173–74. Have you ever witnessed the Holy Spirit moving in a similar way? What was the occasion? How did the experience impact you?

Does the story of Saul's conversion in Acts 9:1–22 resemble the above two incidents? Was the Holy Spirit involved in speaking to Saul and blinding him? How common do you think an experience like Saul's is? Do you think Philip downplays the supernatural too much in this book?

Philip writes, "I sit in a charismatic-style meeting and look around. The music, a few repetitive phrases set to a mediocre composition, jars me but seems to have a mesmerizing effect on others. Their hands lift in the air palms up, their eyes squint shut, their bodies sway. They appear transported to an emotional plane unattainable to me, connecting to something that leaves me behind" (p. 175). How do you respond to Philip's words? Modify any of the following to express, with sensitivity toward others, your own response.

- I too feel this way when others around me are caught up in a physical and seemingly emotional display of worship as Yancey describes. I privately wonder if most of them are just acting a part they feel to be appropriately spiritual.
- Like Yancey, this style of worship just isn't me. I feel no urge to encounter God through such sensual expression. Sometimes I

wonder if I've missed out on something, but usually I feel that the people who worship this way do so simply because they're highly emotional types.

- Interesting to hear Yancey's perspective. For me, this type of moderately charismatic worship is a highlight of my spiritual experience. It helps me block out the world and quiet my own inner noise. It's my time to let God love me and to focus on my love for him.

- Truthfully, people like Yancey bother me. If you can't express your love to God in a physical and emotional way, you're putting serious limits on your intimacy with God. I know personality and spiritual background play into how people worship, but we all have to stretch beyond our comfort zones in one area or another to go deeper with God.

What do you think God finds most pleasing when receiving worship from us? Is he most pleased with a particular style of worship? Does quality of music or presentation matter? Does he see beyond the outward appearance and into the heart?

Philip writes that "any changes God works in a person will come about not as a result of coercion from the outside but by a Spirit working from within, summoning up new life, transforming from the inside out. The words used to describe God's Spirit—Comforter, Helper, Counselor—imply that change may involve a slow, internal process, with many fits and starts." He adds, "Sometimes I secretly yearn for the spectacular . . . when the Holy Spirit chiefly offers a slow, steady progression toward the end God desires all along: the gradual reconstruction of my fallen self" (p. 177).

How do these words reflect God's work in your own life? Looking back, can you see God's Spirit acting as a Comforter, Helper, Counselor in your life? Have you seen a slow, internal process at work, making you gradually into God's image? Thinking of the Holy Spirit from this perspective, do you feel more comfortable with inviting the Spirit to do his work in you?

5. Read the two-paragraph quote by Richard Mouw beginning on the bottom of page 180. Philip writes, "Spiritual powers that hold a person in their grip do not simply disappear, nor do they stay dead. . . . Whether I battle incontinence, an eating disorder, a fear of intimacy, an attraction to lust and infidelity, or a spirit of bitterness and blame, the good news is that I need not 'clean myself up' before approaching God. Just the opposite: in the Spirit, God has found a way to live within me, helping from the inside out. God has not promised a state of constant bliss or a problem-free existence but has promised to be present in the silence and in the dark, to exist alongside us, within us, and for us."

Does this perspective give you new hope for fighting personal battles? Have you ever felt that if a personal problem or weakness wasn't healed within a certain time frame, it would never be healed? Are you content to let God heal and change you slowly rather than immediately?

How does 2 Timothy 1:6–7 speak to the power of God at work in us even when the change is gradual?

6. Philip writes of an extreme fatalism that concludes we humans need do nothing because the will of God works itself out regardless. "From God's perspective, if I may speculate, the great advance in human history may be what happened at Pentecost, which restored the direct correspondence of spirit to Spirit that had been lost in Eden. I want God to act in direct, impressive, irrefutable ways. He wants to 'share

power' with the likes of me, accomplishing his work through people, not despite them" (p. 182).

When have you expected God to act apart from you, rather than in and through you? Perhaps in healing a relational rift, finding a job, resolving a financial difficulty, handling a parenting challenge? Were you right to expect God's help apart from your involvement? Is it ever appropriate to let God handle a problem without your involvement?

7. Philip writes of his marriage, "Like every starry-eyed newlywed, Janet and I both learned that the wedding ceremony was just the beginning of the process of making love work. Our marriage has hardly been a place of serenity, void of negative emotions. To the contrary, we are more likely to express feelings of anger and disappointment to each other than to anyone else, even when 'outside' forces prompt those feelings. A healthy marriage is not a problem-free place, but it can be a safe place. We know that we will still love each other the next day and the next, and that despite the strain, our love may well soothe the hurt that caused those feelings in the first place." Philip adds that similarly, with God "I sense something of the same pattern at work. . . . God offers a 'safe place' to express ourselves, even the worst parts of ourselves" (p. 183).

If you are married, do you find that the marriage relationship is similar in many ways to a Christian's relationship with God—often filled with challenges and conflict despite a serious commitment and a genuine love? If you are not married, do you have a friendship or family relationship that operates in a similar way? Whether you are married or unmarried, how does Philip's comparison of marriage and Christianity make you feel about the difficulties you experience in relating to God?

Do you have any prayer needs to share with the group?

GRASPING FOR UNDERSTANDING OF MYSELF, MY GOD (10–20 MINUTES OR MORE)

So far in the several weeks of study we have completed, we have done much inner examination. We have looked honestly and deeply into many facets of ourselves and our lives. Today rather than doing a directed examination, we will take time to let God speak to us about the work he desires to do in us.

Turn to pages 178–79 and review the bulleted points Philip recorded during a spiritual retreat. Quiet yourself and your surroundings and begin to write your own "spiritual action plan." Do this during several minutes together now as a group (knowing you will need more personal time later to finish), or schedule a time this week for a personal getaway or an in-house retreat to write your action plan. Don't feel a need for eloquent or profound words. However, try to go deeper than simple statements such as "Have a daily quiet time." Listen to the voice that speaks distinctly about the peculiarities of you that get in the way of a full life with God.

CLINGING TO GOD DESPITE THE DISTANCE (5–10 MINUTES)

Now we will spend a few minutes in the sort of prayer we talked about in this session—a prayer in which we will not speak to God but will let God speak to us, telling us good things about ourselves. Remember Nouwen's words: "The real 'work' of prayer is to become silent and listen to the voice that says good things about me."

Close your eyes and, without words, focus your mind on God's love for you. What about you does God delight in? How does God want to encourage you? How intensely must God care for you as his dear child? If a picture will help you focus on God's love, imagine yourself as the prodigal child being welcomed home into the embrace of God, your ecstatic and loving Father. Relax in his embrace and receive his love.

LONGING FOR GOD IN THE WEEK AHEAD (OPTIONAL)

You can integrate this study into your life throughout the week by using the following suggestions and readings.

- This week be mindful of the practice of *statio,* making a conscious effort to pause often between activities and reflect on what you just finished or what you are about to do. As you do this, consider how this practice might transform you.

- In prayer times this week, focus more on letting God love you than on presenting requests, expressing gratitude, or confessing.
- Reflect on these Bible passages in the week ahead as your time allows.
  Day 1: Romans 12:1–8
  Day 2: Colossians 3:1–17
  Day 3: 1 John 4:7–21
  Day 4: 1 Peter 1:3–9
  Day 5: John 15:1–17

The following excerpt is taken from *Life of the Beloved* by Henri Nouwen.

The blessings that we give to each other are expressions of the blessing that rests on us from all eternity. It is the deepest affirmation of our true self. It is not enough to be chosen. We also need an ongoing blessing that allows us to hear in an ever-new way that we belong to a loving God who will never leave us alone, but will remind us always that we are guided by love on every step of our lives. . . .

If the blessing speaks the truth and the curse speaks lies about who you and I are, we are faced with the very concrete question: How to hear and claim the blessing? If the fact of our blessedness is not just a sentiment, but a truth that shapes our daily lives, we must be able to see and experience this blessing in an unambiguous way. Let me offer you two suggestions for claiming your blessedness. These have to do with prayer and presence. [We will not include the section on "presence" in this excerpt.]

First of all, prayer. For me personally, prayer becomes more and more a way to listen to the blessing. I have read and written much about prayer, but when I go to a quiet place to pray, I realize that, although I have a tendency to say many things to God, the real "work" of prayer is to become silent and listen to the voice that says good things about me. This might sound self-indulgent, but, in practice, it is a hard discipline. I am so afraid of being cursed, of hearing that I am no good or not good enough, that I quickly give in to the temptation to start talking and to keep talking in order to control my fears. To gently push aside and silence the many voices that question my goodness and to trust that I will hear a voice of blessing . . . that demands a real effort.

Have you ever tried to spend a whole hour doing nothing but listening to the voice that dwells deep in your heart? When there is no radio to listen to, no TV to watch, no book to read, no person to talk to, no project to finish, no phone call to make, how does that make you feel? Often it does no more than make us so aware of how much there is still to do that we haven't yet done that we decide to leave the fearful silence and go back to work! It is not easy to enter into the silence and reach beyond the many boisterous and demanding voices of our world and to discover there the small intimate voice saying: "You are my Beloved Child, on you my favor rests." Still, if we dare to embrace our solitude and befriend our silence, we will come to know that voice. I do not want to suggest to you that one day you will hear that voice with your bodily ears. I am not speaking about a hallucinatory voice, but about a voice that can be heard by the ear of faith, the ear of the inner heart.

Often you will feel that nothing happens in your prayer. You say: "I am just sitting there and getting distracted." But if you develop the discipline of spending one half-hour a day listening to the voice of love, you will gradually discover that something is happening of which you were not even conscious. It might be only in retrospect that you discover the voice that blesses you. You thought that what happened during your time of listening was nothing more than a lot of confusion, but then you discover yourself looking forward to your quiet time and missing it when you can't have it. The movement of God's Spirit is very gentle, very soft—and hidden. It does not seek attention. But that movement is also very persistent, strong and deep. It changes our hearts radically. The faithful discipline of prayer reveals to you that you are the blessed one and gives you the power to bless others.

It might be helpful here to offer a concrete suggestion. One good way to listen is to listen with a sacred text: a psalm or a prayer, for instance. The Hindu spiritual writer Eknath Easwaran showed me the great value of learning a sacred text by heart and repeating it slowly in the mind, word by word, sentence by sentence. In this way, listening to the voice of love becomes not just a passive waiting, but an active attentiveness to the voice that speaks to us through the words of the Scriptures.

I spent many of my half-hours of prayer doing nothing but slowly repeating the prayer of St. Francis: "Lord make me an instrument of your peace. Where there is hatred let me show love. . . ." As I let these words move from my mind to my heart, I began to experience, beyond all my restless emotions and feelings, the peace and love I was asking for in words.

In this way I also had a way to deal with my endless distractions. When I found myself wandering away far and wide, I could always return to my simple prayer and thereby listen again in my heart to the voice I so much wanted to hear.[1]

PASSION AND GOD'S PRESENCE

—⁂—

The excerpt below is from *Reaching for the Invisible God.*

Chart out a course that guarantees a successful prayer life, the active presence of God, and constant victory over temptation, and you will probably run aground. A relationship with an invisible God will always include uncertainty and variability.

As I look back over the giants of faith, all had one thing in common: neither victory nor success, but *passion*. An emphasis on spiritual technique may well lead us away from the passionate relationship that God values above all. More than a doctrinal system, more than a mystical experience, the Bible emphasizes a relationship with a Person, and personal relationships are never steady-state.

God's favorites responded with passion in kind. Moses argued with God so fervently that several times he persuaded God to change his mind. Jacob wrestled all night long and used trickery to grab hold of God's blessing. Job lashed out in sarcastic rage against God. David broke at least half the Ten Commandments. Yet never did they wholly give up on God, and never did God give up on them. God can handle anger, blame, and even willful disobedience. One thing, however, blocks relationship: indifference. "They turned their backs to me and not their faces," God told Jeremiah, in a damning indictment of Israel.

Adult Children of Alcoholics, an organization that works with families afflicted by alcoholism, identifies three coping mechanisms children learn in order to survive such a dysfunctional setting: Don't Talk, Don't

Trust, and Don't Feel. Later, as adults, these same survivors find them-selves incapable of sustaining an intimate relationship and must unlearn the pattern of indifference. Christian counselors tell me that wounded Christians may relate to God in the same way. Reacting against a strict upbringing or feeling betrayed by God, they squelch all passion and fall back on a more formal, less personal faith.

From the spiritual giants of the Bible, I learn this crucial lesson about relating to an invisible God: Whatever you do, don't ignore God. Invite God into every aspect of life. For some Christians, the times of Job-like crisis will represent the greatest danger. How can they cling to faith in a God who appears unconcerned and even hostile? Others, and I count myself among them, face a more subtle danger. An accumulation of dis-tractions gradually edges God away from the center of my life. Some days I meet people, eat, work, make decisions, all without giving God a single thought. And that void is far more serious than what Job experi-enced, for not once did Job stop thinking about God.

I keep thumbing back to the story of David because I know no better model for a passionate relationship with God than the king named David. His very name meant, appropriately, "beloved."

David's secret? Two scenes, one a buoyant high and the other a dev-astating low, hint at an answer. Whether cartwheeling behind the ark (2 Samuel 6) or lying prostrate on the ground for six straight nights in contrition [after his murder and adultery] (2 Samuel 12), David's strongest instinct was to relate his life to God. In comparison, nothing else mattered at all. As his poetry makes clear, he led a God-saturated life. "O God, you are my God, earnestly I seek you," he wrote once in a des-iccated desert. "My soul thirsts for you, my body longs for you, in a dry and weary land where there is no water. . . . Because your love is better than life, my lips will glorify you."

I assumed that spiritual maturity would progress like physical matura-tion. A baby learns to crawl, then toddle like a drunk, and then run. Should not our walk with God progress the same way, so that we grad-ually strengthen, gain control of our early lurching motions, and then stride toward sainthood? Listen, though, to the sequence in a familiar passage from Isaiah:

Those who hope in the Lord
   will renew their strength.
They will soar on wings like eagles;
    they will run and not grow weary,
    they will walk and not be faint.

John Claypool, reflecting on that passage, notes that the order reverses what we might expect. As if to overturn our preconceptions, Isaiah begins with soaring and ends with walking. All Christians pass through various stages. At times—for many it comes early in the journey—we soar in a state of spiritual ecstasy; at times we run, expressing our faith with the boundless energy of activism; at times we can barely take a step without fainting.

⌀

I have mentioned that distractions can push God away from the center of my life—in truth, they push God out of my field of consciousness altogether. It amazes me how I can sail through my daily routine without giving God much thought or putting into practice what I write.

I marvel at a God who puts himself at our mercy, as it were, allowing himself to be quenched and grieved, and even forgotten. Reading the Old Testament convinces me that this human tendency—indifference taken to a lethal extreme—bothers God more than any other. Gracious to doubters and a pursuer of willful unbelievers, God finds himself stymied, and even enraged, by those who simply put him out of mind. God reacts like any spurned lover who finds his phone calls unreturned and his Valentines tossed aside unopened.

"Only be careful, and watch yourselves closely so that you do not forget . . . ," Moses warned the Israelites as he introduced some visual reminders of the covenant. A short time later, though, he faced up to the reality: "Your heart will become proud and you will forget the Lord your God, who brought you out of Egypt, out of the land of slavery." The Israelites' forgetfulness developed just as Moses predicted.

⌀

How can we avoid the amnesia of the Israelites? Over the years I have tried various ways to "remember" God. For me, the process divides into a daily habit of reorientation and conscious remembering.

Reorientation for me means beginning the day with a God-consciousness so that gradually the center of my thought moves from self to God. I used to jump out of bed as soon as I woke up. Now I lie there in the quiet and invite God into my day, not as a participant in my life or an item on a check list but as the hub of all that will happen that day. I want God to become the central reality, so that I am as aware of God as I am of my own moods and desires.

The first great commandment requires us to love God, which we do best through awareness of his great love for us. Thomas Merton remarks, "The 'remembering' of God, of which we sing in the Psalms, is simply the rediscovery, in deep compunction of heart, that God remembers us."

Throughout the day, I need aids for conscious remembering. For a while I tried setting my watch alarm to chime at the top of each hour. I would stop what I was doing, reflect on the hour that had just passed, and strive to practice the presence of God during the next hour. Later I learned I had accidentally stumbled on an old technique of Benedictine monks, who would stop and say the hour prayer every time the clock chimed. With the help of such markers during the day, remembering God can gradually become something of a habit.

I have also learned about conscious remembering from Brother Lawrence, a cook in a seventeenth-century monastery who wrote the devotional classic *The Practice of the Presence of God*. Brother Lawrence mentions practical ways to "offer God your heart from time to time in the course of the day," even in the midst of chores, "to savor him, though it be but in passing, and as it were by stealth." The depth of spirituality, said Lawrence, does not depend on changing things you do but rather in doing for God what you ordinarily do for yourself. Lawrence shied away from spiritual retreats because he found it as easy to worship God in his common tasks as in the desert.

A Christian who lived in our own century strove throughout his life to put Brother Lawrence's principles into practice. Worldwide, Frank Laubach gained renown as the founder of the modern literacy movement, the person who has probably done more than anyone in history to teach people to read and write. His private journals, however, record a lifelong effort to make a different kind of mark: to live in constant awareness of God's presence.

After a year he could report, "This simple practice requires only a gentle pressure of the will, not more than a person can exert easily. It grows easier as the habit becomes fixed. Yet it transforms life into heaven."

Gradually, though, he found that the daily exercise transformed his spirit. Every time he met a person, he inwardly prayed for the other party. Answering the telephone, he would whisper to himself, "A child of God will now speak to me." Walking down a street or standing in line at a bus stop, he would pray silently for the people around him.

Laubach proves that one can combine a busy, modern life with mysticism; we need not seclude ourselves in a monastery or convent. He served as Dean of Education at a major university, helped found a seminary, worked among tribal people, served the poor, and traveled worldwide to promote his literacy techniques.

It does not do justice to Brother Lawrence or Frank Laubach to report snatches of a lifelong process. If their spiritual exercises seem like hard work performed under a sense of obligation, read their full accounts. For them, the discipline led to delight and joy. They simply recognized that the oddity of a personal relationship between an infinite, invisible being and a finite, visible one requires certain adjustments.

As Laubach reports, the reward fully compensates the effort: "After months and years of practicing the presence of God, one feels that God is closer; His push from behind seems to be stronger and steadier, and the pull from in front seems to grow stronger. . . . God is so close then that He not only lives all around us, but all *through* us."

I now hear the phrase "practicing the presence of God" in a different way. Previously I sought an emotional confirmation that God is actually there. Sometimes I have that sense, sometimes I do not. I have changed the emphasis, though, to one of putting myself in God's presence. I assume God is present all around me, though undetectable by my senses, and strive to conduct my daily life in a way appropriate to God's presence. Can I refer back to God whatever happens today, as a kind of offering?

ENCOUNTERING GOD THROUGH THOSE IN THE BIBLE (5 MINUTES)

Read the following stories of King David, using the accompanying introductions before the reading of each Scripture passage.

2 Samuel 6:1–23. The ark of the covenant, a chest made of acacia wood, measured roughly four feet long by two feet high. Covered with gold inside and out, it proclaimed a holy function. Two cherubim sat atop the cover with wings outspread, as if guarding the two tablets containing the Ten Commandments housed inside. The ark represented the presence of God, who, in Old Testament times, lived among his chosen people. As this story begins, the ark has been separated from the tabernacle and other places of worship for one hundred years, even held briefly by the opposing Philistines. Finally David has recognized the importance of building a spiritual as well as religious capital of the kingdom of Israel. He has designated Jerusalem that place, and at last brings the ark to rest inside the tabernacle in Jerusalem.

2 Samuel 12:1–13. This story takes place just after Bathsheba becomes King David's wife. In brief, David saw Bathsheba bathing from his rooftop and called her to his quarters. Bathsheba became pregnant and, after David brought her husband home from war and unsuccessfully tempted him to sleep with her and legitimize the baby, David plotted to bring on Uriah's death at the front lines of battle. David coveted, committed adultery, lied, and murdered. Now the prophet Nathan must convey God's displeasure.

REACHING FOR GOD WITH OTHERS (25 MINUTES)

If you are in a large group, break into groups of four to six for this discussion time. Introduce yourselves to each other if necessary. Share briefly with the others: What is the last passionate thing you can recall doing today or in the last couple of days? Maybe something simple like giving a friend, child, or spouse a spontaneous hug or kiss. Maybe a passionate conversation you had. Maybe a letter you wrote or a song you sang in the shower. Maybe a spontaneous gift or favor to a neighbor.

1. We are now more than halfway through this study of Philip's book. What is your take on the book so far? Has the book disturbed you? Struck a chord? Validated longtime frustrations? Fallen short of expressing what God has meant to you? Shaken your faith? Disillusioned you toward Christianity? Left you with much to ponder?

Most likely this book, because of its honesty about spiritual struggles, is making all of us think deeply about our views of God, our expectations, and our daily habits in pursuing him. Would you agree that the more each of us is disturbed or provoked or relieved as we consider these themes, the more indication we have that we feel passionately about God? Why or why not?

Does your passion, whether in the form of struggle with God or love for God, seem to drive you toward God or away from him? Has this study so far brought you closer to God or caused you to feel more distant from him? Do you have an idea why this is so?

2. Review the quote by Henri Nouwen on pages 185–86. Do Nouwen's words surprise you? Do they disturb you? Have you ever felt the same way? Why is it unsettling to think of a spiritual leader struggling this way?

Thomas Green, spiritual director and specialist in prayer, says dryness is the normal outcome of a life of prayer. He draws a parallel with human love, comparing life with God to the stages of courtship, honeymoon, and mature love. As with human love, the last stage with God involves more tedium than romance. Thus a season of dryness in prayer might signify growth, not failure. Does this idea make sense to you, or would you contend that the more spiritually mature a person is, the more intimate his or her prayer life will be? In a season of dryness, what should a person do? Seek to be content and wait it out? Or continue seeking a renewed sense of intimacy with God?

3. Philip writes, "As I look back over the giants of faith, all had one thing in common: neither victory nor success, but *passion*. . . . God can handle anger, blame, and even willful disobedience. One thing, however, blocks relationship: indifference. . . . From the spiritual giants of the Bible, I learn this crucial lesson about relating to an invisible God: Whatever you do, don't ignore God. Invite God into every aspect of your life" (pp. 188–89).

Moses argued fervently with God and changed his mind, Jacob wrestled with God and used trickery to gain God's blessing, Job raged at God, David broke half the Ten Commandments. When have you acted in a way similar to that of these well-loved men of the Bible? Did you worry, at the time or later, that God would reject you because of your behavior? What do you think about it now? Is Philip suggesting that sinful behavior is okay, as long as you're relating to God in some way?

Philip continues, "For some Christians, the times of Job-like crisis will represent the greatest danger. How can they cling to faith in a God who appears unconcerned and even hostile? Others . . . face a more subtle danger. An accumulation of distractions . . . gradually edges God away from the center of my life" (p. 189). Which is or has been the greater danger for you? Are you more prone to forget about God during the hard times? Or do daily distractions pose more of a threat to your God-consciousness?

4. Turn back to the stories of King David in 2 Samuel. As noted in the introduction to the first story, David put much effort into establishing Jerusalem as the spiritual capital of the kingdom of Israel. He

worked hard to make a place where God was central and the nation's spiritual foundation was recognized. Do you think this work and commitment had an impact on the great passion David felt in bringing the ark to Jerusalem?

Do you think that, as with David, the more intentionally you seek to make a place for God in your life, the more passion you will feel for him? Why or why not?

Now look at the second story about David. In this story, as well as in the previous story, David clearly demonstrates a fear of, or great respect for, the Lord. How is this fear evident in each story? What connection might such a fear of God have with a person's passion for God?

Read Psalm 63:1–3. Do you feel a passion for God similar to the kind of passion David felt? During those times in your life when you do not feel this passion, what might help to restore or create such a passion?

5. Philip writes about a friend, Bud, who works among drug addicts. "I've decided there is one key in determining whether individual drug addicts can be cured: if they deeply believe they are a *forgivable* child of God. Not a failure-free child of God, a forgivable one," says Bud (p. 193). Why would this belief be key in overcoming an addiction?

Can you recall a time in your life when you struggled to overcome a problem of your own making? Share the details as you are able. Did you come to a place of honest repentance before God? How important was your repentance and your belief in forgiveness to your eventual healing?

6. As you look back on your life as a Christian, when were you most passionate about God: in your early days as a believer, later as you began to grow in your faith, or much later after you had known Jesus for many years? If you've been most passionate in the later stages of your faith, has the passion surfaced as you have sought a more daily, intimate relationship with God? Or can you distinguish between different types of passion—maybe a great excitement and fervor in the early days versus a quieter yet deeper and more mature passion in the later days?

How have you felt during those times when the passion was not there? Worried? Panicky? Unsure you are saved? Apathetic? Uncertain you really need Christianity?

Philip writes, "I assumed that spiritual maturity would progress like physical maturation. A baby learns to crawl, then toddle like a drunk, and then run. Should not our walk with God progress the same way, so that we gradually strengthen, gain control of our early lurching motions, and then stride toward sainthood?" (p. 199). Read Isaiah 40:31, printed at the bottom of page 199.

"As if to overturn our preconceptions, Isaiah begins with soaring and ends with walking," Philip continues, citing John Claypool.

"At times—for many it comes early in the journey—we soar in a state of spiritual ecstasy; at times we run, expressing our faith with the boundless energy of activism; at times we can barely take a step without fainting" (p. 200).

Do you find this backward progression of Isaiah's true in your own life? When have you experienced a drop-off from running with the boundless energy of activism to barely walking without fainting? When this happened, did you experience guilt over your lack of desire or ability to actively serve, care for others, or better the world? Do you think God requires service of us when we are in these periods of barely walking ourselves? Why or why not?

How might Isaiah's promise (that we will walk and not faint) take on new meaning for those dark times of faith? (See the quote by John Claypool in the middle of page 200.)

7. Philip confesses, "It amazes me how I can sail through [my] daily routine without giving God much thought or putting into practice what I write" (p. 200). If you are honest with yourself and others, how true of you is Philip's statement? Is God a frequent part of your consciousness or more of an occasional or oft-forgotten thought?

Have you developed any routines or aids in keeping God more frequently in mind? If so, what are they? Has any trial or life event made a difference in how much God is a conscious part of your days?

Philip writes, "We remember God best by believing that we *matter*, personally and infinitely, to him." Why is this core knowledge so necessary for remembering God daily and hourly?

8. Review the stories of Brother Lawrence and Frank Laubach on pages 204–7. Have you ever, or do you now, "practice the presence of God"? How practical does this practice seem to you? If you have tried it, how difficult did you find it? What difference did it make for you?

Laubach wrote, "My will-pressure must be gentle but constant, to listen to God, to pray for others incessantly, to look at people as souls and not clothes, or bodies, or even minds. . . . 'Let go and let God' does not fit my experience. 'Take hold and keep hold of God' is what it feels like to me." Laubach served as dean of a major university, helped found a seminary, worked among tribal people and the poor, and taught literacy techniques worldwide. In light of Laubach's busyness and involvement in the world, do you think such a practice as his would be possible in your life? Why or why not?

If you have not tried practicing the presence of God as Brother Lawrence and Frank Laubach did, what difference do you think it might make in your life?

Do you have any prayer needs to share with the group?

GRASPING FOR UNDERSTANDING OF MYSELF, MY GOD (10 – 20 MINUTES OR MORE)

Today we will dig deeper in an attempt to find the roots of our personal passion and detect any poisons that may be keeping our passion for God from flourishing. Imagine yourself digging with your hands deeper and deeper into the soil, which is your spiritual life. Your passion lies within the soil. Consider these questions as you dig.

- Children of alcoholics learn that survival requires they don't talk, don't trust, and don't feel. They turn off the parts of themselves that are needed for intimacy with others. Has anything in your background prompted you to cease talking, trusting, or feeling? If so, do you struggle in building intimacy with others?

- Some people from dysfunctional backgrounds react in an opposite way. Out of a reservoir of unmet need, they cannot stop talking, they seek to trust those who are not trustworthy, and they experience an overflow of feelings they can't control. Does this pattern fit you?

- Wounded Christians may respond to God in either of the above ways. A strict upbringing, a bad experience in a charismatic community, or a sense of betrayal by God may squelch all passion toward God and cause a person to practice a more formal, less personal faith that lacks passionate response to God. Do you see yourself in this description?

- A wounded Christian might also respond to God with extreme passion and an overflow of emotion. Lack of passion may never be a problem. Rather the challenge may come in rightly directing that passion and in accepting the paradoxes, or unanswered questions, inherent in faith in God. Do you see yourself in this description?

- How do distractions affect your passion for God? Does the stuff of daily life—deadlines, to-do lists, phone calls, errands, housekeeping, parenting, commuting—gradually edge God from the center of your life? How often does a day go by with hardly a thought of God?

- What kind of poison is most threatening to your passion for God: the poison of a response to your wounded past that keeps you from passionately living out your love for God, or the more subtle and seemingly innocent poison of distractions that make you forget God?

- If you are fighting the poison of past wounds, what could help you to heal from those wounds and then begin remaking yourself so passion can live again within your relationship with God?
- If you are fighting the poison of daily distractions, do you have a sense of how much your inattention grieves God? What needs to change in your life to make you less prone to forgetting God? What needs to change in your spiritual life to help you remember God throughout the unchangeable duties of each day?

CLINGING TO GOD DESPITE THE DISTANCE (5 – 10 MINUTES)

Now we will sit quietly with God for a few minutes and focus on practicing the presence of God. Close your eyes and imagine yourself in the atmosphere in which you spend most of your days (at your desk at work, in your home, in the car, on the phone, etc.). Watch yourself as if from above, and as you watch, see also the presence of the Spirit of God hovering next to you in everything you are doing. Listen to Brother Lawrence's words:

> He does not ask much of us—an occasional remembrance, a small act of worship, now to beg his grace, at times to offer him our distresses, at another time to render thanks for the favors he has given, and which he gives in the midst of your labors, to find consolation with him as often as you can. At table and in the midst of conversation, lift your heart at times toward him. The smallest remembrance will always please him. It is not needful at such times to cry out loud. He is nearer to us than we think.

Imagine yourself doing as Brother Lawrence suggests, asking for God's help as you work at your desk on a difficult assignment, telling him about your distress over a financial worry as you pay a bill, thanking him for the kind words of a friend on the phone, thinking of God as you eat a meal with your family. In those tasks you especially dislike, imagine yourself offering your activity to God as a gift of love to him.

Now remember what Frank Laubach encourages. Listen to God, pray for others incessantly, look at people as souls and not as clothes or bodies or even minds. Take hold and keep hold of God. Imagine yourself, as you go about your day, thinking this way. Pray that God would help you to do in the coming days as you are imagining now.

Longing for God in the Week Ahead (Optional)

You can integrate this study into your life throughout the week by using the following suggestions and readings.

- This week be intentional about practicing the presence of God. In bed each morning, center your thoughts on God, beginning the practice you will carry through the day: that of turning your mind often to God, whispering silent words of thanks, need, and love, and simply enjoying the awareness that God is with you.
- Reflect on these Bible passages in the week ahead as your time allows.
  Day 1: Genesis 27:1–40
  Day 2: Genesis 32:22–32
  Day 3: Exodus 32:1–16
  Day 4: Job 3:1–26
  Day 5: Psalm 51

The following excerpt is from the book *Prayer: Finding the Heart's True Home* by Richard Foster.

Unceasing Prayer is associated with such practitioners of prayer as Brother Lawrence *(The Practice of the Presence of God)*, Thomas Kelly *(A Testament of Devotion)*, and Frank Laubach *(Letters by a Modern Mystic)*. Their profoundly simple approach is to go through all the activities of our days in joyful awareness of God's presence with whispered prayers of praise and adoration flowing continuously from our hearts. Brother Lawrence, who called himself "the lord of all pots and pans," crystallized this idea in his now-famous comment "the time of business does not with me differ from the time of prayer; and in the noise and clatter of my kitchen, while several persons are at the same time calling for different things, I possess God in as great tranquility as if I were upon my knees at the blessed sacrament."

Lawrence urges us to "make a private chapel of our heart where we can retire from time to time to commune with Him, peacefully, humbly, lovingly." He encourages us to make inward prayer the last act of the evening and the first act of the morning and in so doing discover that "those who have been breathed on by the Holy Spirit move forward even while sleeping."

In the latter years of his short life philosopher Thomas Kelly tells us that "the wells of living water of divine revelation rise up continuously, day by day and hour by hour, steady and transfiguring." He writes, "There is a way of ordering our mental life on more than one level at once. On one level we may be thinking, discussing, seeing, calculating, meeting all the demands of external affairs. But deep within, behind the scenes, at a profounder level, we may also be in prayer and adoration, song and worship and a gentle receptiveness to divine breathings."

The many diary notations of Frank Laubach are radiant with the Shekinah of God: "This afternoon the possession of God has caught me up with such sheer joy that I thought I never had known anything like it. God was so close and so amazingly lovely that I felt like melting all over with a strange blissful contentment." In 1930 on the tiny Philippine island of Mindanao he writes, "This sense of cooperation with God in little things is what so astonishes me, for I never have felt it this way before. . . . My part is to live this hour in continuous inner conversation with God and in perfect responsiveness to his will. To make this hour gloriously rich. This seems to be all I need think about." Several years later and on another continent he prays, "God, this attempt to keep my *will* bent toward Your will is integrating me. Here in this Calcutta station, I feel new power such as I have not had for many years."

I am at a loss to convey to you the sense of immediacy, of adventure, of breakthrough that is in the journals and letters not only of these three but also of many other pioneers in the spiritual life. These people were alive to a reality that most of us miss. Their writings dance with the excitement of discovery. Thomas Kelly writes, "Life from the Center is a life of unhurried peace and power. It is simple. It is serene. It is amazing. It is triumphant. It is radiant. It takes no time, but it occupies all our time. And it makes our life programs new and overcoming."[1]

MATURING IN
THE FAITH

The excerpt below is from *Reaching for the Invisible God*.

I have known God's presence and God's absence, fullness and emptiness, spiritual intimacy and a dark void. The sequence as well as the vari-
ety of these steps in my pilgrimage took me by surprise, and as I looked
around for a road map that might offer clues on what to expect, I found
much confusion.

Some groups of Christians equate spiritual maturity and asceticism:
whoever keeps the strictest rules gains intimacy with God. This cannot
be correct, I know, because Jesus himself had a loose reputation compared to John the Baptist or the Pharisees.

Other Christians devalue the search for intimacy with God. I have
friends serving on the front lines of justice issues who scorn spiritual disciplines as "too mystical." Although I admire their commitment and
agree with some of their causes, I cannot simply ignore the many biblical passages on union with God and on the need for holiness. What
then does a mature Christian look like? And how does my behavior affect
a relationship with God?

With these issues in mind I slowly read the entire New Testament,
marking on a yellow legal pad every passage that encouraged believers
to grow spiritually. The New Testament presents life with God as a journey, with followers found at many different places along the way. For
the sake of convenience I settled on three rough groupings—Child,

Adult, and Parent. These three categories summarized for me three over-all stages in the spiritual life. First, I looked at all the passages directed to Christians who were just beginning their pilgrimage or who seemed stuck in the Child stage.

A surprising number of passages earned a "Child" in the margin for their approach. Like parents do with children, Jesus did not hesitate to threaten dire punishment for the disobedient and promise rewards to the obedient. Some behavior is so harmful that we simply must avoid it.

New Testament writers cannot comprehend why some believers lag in perpetual adolescence when they should be acting like adults. Although they may prefer appealing to "higher" motives, these authors go ahead and spell out the scary consequences of wrong behavior, for they know that a wise choice out of immature motives beats a poor choice.

———— ❧ ————

On the other hand, Jesus plainly stated that "unless you change and become like little children, you will never enter the kingdom of heaven." Somehow we must learn to distinguish between appropriate *childlike* behavior, a prerequisite for the kingdom of heaven, and inappropriate *childish* behavior, a mark of stunted growth.

While I still bear the scars of growing pains, I am learning to iden-tify and avoid some seductions of childish faith: unrealistic expectations, legalism, and unhealthy dependence.

Several times I have alluded to the danger of unrealistic expectations. A child must, at some point, learn to accept the world as it is rather than as he or she wants it to be.

According to both Jesus and Paul, legalism represents another symp-tom of childish faith. As Paul explained it, the strictness of the Old Tes-tament law was intended not to offer an alternative path to God, rather to prove that no amount of strictness can achieve what God desires. God wants perfection, and for that we need another way, the way of grace.

Looking back on Old Testament times, Paul also saw a pattern of unhealthy dependence. Like children reared by a famous parent who provides for all their needs, the Israelites found their identity by resent-ing their dependence on God. They stayed in a state of childish rebellion whereas God wanted them to move steadily toward adulthood.

A childish faith based on unrealistic expectations, legalism, and unhealthy dependence can work well for a while—until a person runs headfirst into a new reality. Job broke through that barrier, as did Abraham, the prophets, and Jesus' disciples. "Lazarus is dead," Jesus told his disciples, "and for your sake I am glad I was not there, so that you may believe." He was preparing them for a new reality that included resurrection, yes, but not before the necessary step of death.

———— ໐⅏໐ ————

Tucked away in a sermon by Frederick Buechner, I find three traits of childhood that may well hint at the meaning of childlike, as opposed to childish, faith.

Children, says Buechner, have no fixed preconceptions of reality. "They don't know any better," we say of children who believe in magic and pretend playmates.

The faith that astonished Jesus had a disturbingly childlike quality, and as I read the Gospels I am convicted of my own lack of childlike faith. Too easily I settle for lowered expectations, holding out little hope of change, not believing that God can heal wounds in me that I have learned to live with. The balance between childlike and childish faith may be precarious, but we dare not tilt too far toward the one in trying to avoid the other.

Second, says Buechner, children know how to accept a gift. Dependent since birth, they receive gladly and unselfconsciously.

Children have taught me most of what I know about praise and thanksgiving. They have no problem giving thanks every day for the family dog and the squirrels who play outside. Only a childlike spirit allows me to receive God's ordinary gifts each day without thinking them ordinary. And the same childlike spirit allows me to open my hands to God's grace, which comes to me free of charge, unrelated to my performance.

Third, children know how to trust. A busy street holds no terror for a child who has an adult's hand to grasp. Indeed, children must sternly be taught *not* to trust strangers, for distrust goes against their instincts.

———— ໐⅏໐ ————

Wise parents nudge their children away from dependence toward freedom, for their goal is to produce independent adults. Lovers, however, choose a new kind of voluntary dependence: possessing freedom, they gladly give it away. In a healthy marriage, one partner yields to the other's wishes not out of compulsion but out of love. That adult relationship reveals, I believe, what God has always sought from human beings: not the clinging, helpless love of a child who has no real choice, but the mature, freely given commitment of a lover.

Marriage offers only one sure check on freedom abuse: love. In any mature relationship, in fact, love sets the boundaries. In my own marriage of thirty years I could point to many times in which Janet has set aside her own first preferences in favor of mine, and I have done the same for her. Neither of us "wins" all the time. Yet because we are committed to each other, we make the small and large adjustments necessary to live together in peace, and try to exercise power and freedom within the boundaries marked by love.

Lovers understand that a lasting relationship grows in the soil of trust and grace and forgiveness, not law. Lovers know that love cannot be commanded or compelled. By nature a lover wants what the other person wants. When love requires personal sacrifice, it often seems more like a gift: "Not my will but thine be done." Lovers praise: I talk about my wife to others and boast of her accomplishments not because I feel obligated but because I want others to know her as I do. In these and other ways, I have learned from marriage how a mature relationship with God may work. Augustine described a good spiritual life as, simply, "well-ordered love."

The state God wants only comes about as a result of a faithful relationship with him. We seek to please God, accept as our highest goal to know and love him, make necessary sacrifices—and in the process we ourselves change. Personal spirituality grows as a byproduct of sustained interaction with God. In the end, we find ourselves not just doing things that please God but wanting to do them.

———— ❧ ————

Jesus told of a merchant who found one pearl so incomparable that he sold everything he owned in order to buy it. The joy in what he gained swallowed up any remorse in what he lost. That is the Adult image of the Christian life: not a grim-faced regimen of self-discipline but an exuberant new life easily worth whatever sacrifice may be required.

Attaining that goal may take time and practice, of course. As C. S. Lewis said, "I must say my prayers today whether I feel devout or not; but that is only as I must learn my grammar if I am ever to read the poets."

Reading the New Testament, I am struck by how consistently the authors appeal to my new identity as a motive for good behavior. As a temple of the living God, what business have I rooting around in what I know God disapproves of? Henri Nouwen calls this new identity "the inner voice of love," an indwelling reminder that frees me to act as God's beloved, beyond the reach of human praise or blame. Goodness, or "holiness," is not some egregious new routine that I must lace around myself like a hair shirt. It is the outworking of an inner transformation, the gradual but sure response of a person in whom God lives.

———⌘———

I feel unqualified to give anyone specific instructions in spiritual disciplines. Rather, I recommend recent works by Eugene Peterson, Dallas Willard, and Richard Foster; Thomas Merton's instructions of a generation ago; and the detailed programs set out by Benedict and Ignatius in past centuries. Simplicity, solitude, submission, service, confession, worship, meditation, prayer, fasting, study, spiritual direction, Sabbath-keeping, pilgrimage, small groups, stewardship, journal-keeping, purity, friendship, devotion, work, leadership, witness—all these may play a role in spiritual maturity, and all of them require a commitment that draws on the old-fashioned notion of discipline.

As I study people like Merton, Benedict, Francis of Assisi, John Wesley, Charles de Foucauld, Mother Teresa, I see in these disciplined souls not set-jaw determination but rather spontaneity and even joy. By investing their freedom in discipline, they secure a deeper freedom unavailable elsewhere.

Love is what God wants from a relationship with us, but we humans tend to experience love like any emotion: intermittently, waxing and waning. Discipline nurtures in us a spiritual staying power—the kind of love a couple enjoys on their golden anniversary, not at their wedding.

———⌘———

"If you can't fly, run. If you can't run, walk. If you can't walk, crawl, but by all means keep moving," Martin Luther King Jr. used to tell the civil rights workers. His advice applies to Christian pilgrims. Life with God advances like any relationship: unsteadily, with misunderstandings and long periods of silence, with victories and failures, testings and triumphs. To achieve the perfection that drew us on the quest, we must wait until the race has ended, until death, and the waiting itself is an act of extraordinary faith and courage.

ENCOUNTERING GOD THROUGH THOSE IN THE BIBLE (3 – 5 MINUTES)

Read the following Scripture passages.
Hebrews 5:12–6:1
1 John 4:7–18

REACHING FOR GOD WITH OTHERS (25 MINUTES)

Leaders: This session is a particularly long one. We strongly encourage you to consider spending two class periods on these questions and the following exercises so your group can have sufficient time to cover all the material.

If you are in a large group, break into groups of four to six for this discussion time. Introduce yourselves to each other if necessary. Tell the others about one of your favorite pastimes as a child.

1. Can you recall something you did as a teenager that made you feel really grown up? How well did you handle this privilege or freedom? Looking back, was this particular act a good indication of your emerging maturity, or did you still have far to go in claiming adulthood? If you are a parent, does your child do anything, or want to do anything, that makes him or her feel big or grown up?

Philip begins his discussion of spiritual maturity noting the criteria some Christians have given to prove spiritual maturity. Some claim that asceticism, or strict rule-keeping, is the way to intimacy with God. Others claim that a pursuit of social justice is the necessary proof of spiritual maturity. Still others might claim that certain experiences of the Holy Spirit, or work in missions, or membership in a particular church are necessary. Did you identify closely with any of these? What criteria for maturity have you held in the past? What happened as you tried to live by this criteria?

Philip writes, "Jesus himself did not hesitate to threaten dire punishment for the disobedient and promise rewards to the obedient. Some behavior is so harmful that we simply must avoid it. . . . New Testament writers cannot comprehend why some believers lag in perpetual adolescence when they should be acting like adults. Although they may prefer appealing to 'higher motives,' these authors go ahead and spell out the scary consequences of wrong behavior, for they know that a wise choice out of immature motives beats a poor choice" (p. 213).

Has there been a time in your life when you seriously questioned the necessity of one of God's commandments and maybe even disobeyed because you did not feel this command was beneficial for your life? Share with the others as you are able. Did anyone challenge you on your choices at the time? Did you ever reach a point where you found you'd been wrong and should have obeyed after all? What did you learn from this experience?

Considering the above question, how does a spiritually mature person view God's commands? What does Hebrews 5:12–6:1 have to say about this?

2. Read the quote by J. I. Packer on pages 215–16. Did you experience what he describes regarding young Christians? When did you begin to feel part of a "tougher school" in your Christian life?

3. Philip discusses three indications of a childish faith: unrealistic expectations, legalism, and unhealthy dependence. What unrealistic expectations have you had to relinquish about the way Christianity should

work? (Perhaps "name it and claim it" or the notion that God would change the rules and make life easier.) How do we distinguish between unrealistic expectations and strong faith in what God can do?

Has legalism ever threatened your spiritual development, or is it doing so now? Have you ever looked upon strict rule-keeping as a measure of spiritual health or upheld certain rules that would set you a step above other Christians? Has legalism ever pushed you or someone you know toward disobedience rather than obedience?

Are you overly dependent on anyone in your life? Your parents? A good friend? A sibling? Your spouse? Have you ever acted out an unhealthy dependence on God in the form of a childish rebellion against him? Have you focused more on lashing out at God than on taking responsibility for your emotions and working through them with his help? Do you settle for a shallow faith, claiming easy answers for complex questions and avoiding going deeper?

4. Frederick Buechner identified three traits of childlike, as opposed to childish, faith. First, children have no fixed perceptions of reality. They believe beyond what common sense might see. Philip admits, "The faith that astonished Jesus had a disturbingly childlike quality, and as I read the Gospels I am convicted of my own lack of childlike faith. Too easily I settle for lowered expectations, holding out little hope of change, not believing that God can heal wounds in me that I have learned to live with. The balance between childlike and childish faith may be precarious, but we dare not tilt too far toward the one in trying to avoid the other" (p. 218).

Where does your faith stand? Are you more prone to childish or childlike faith?

Second, says Buechner, children know how to accept a gift. "Only a childlike spirit allows me to receive God's ordinary gifts each day without thinking them ordinary," Philip writes. "And the same childlike spirit allows me to open my hands to God's grace, which comes to me free of charge, unrelated to my performance" (p. 219). Are you comfortable receiving gifts? Do God's ordinary gifts each day prompt frequent gratitude, or is it difficult for you to stay aware of the small things and find joy in them? How well do you receive God's grace?

Third, children know how to trust, says Buechner. Quoting Kathleen Norris, Philip writes on page 219 that "doubt is merely the seed of faith, a sign that faith is alive and ready to grow." To have a relationship with God, we must trust as a child and "plunge into it without knowing where it might take [us]" (p. 219). When has doubt kept you from trusting God? Did trusting God feel foolish if you harbored such strong reservations? What do you think of Norris's statement about doubt being the seed of faith? Looking back, has this proven true for you? How does this idea make you feel about your current doubts or those of someone you know?

5. Review the story of Walter Ciszek on pages 220–22. Have you ever, like Ciszek, thought you knew what God's will for you was, only to watch that will fall apart before your eyes? In what situation did you find yourself after God's supposed plans fell apart? Did where you were left seem at all like the vision you thought you'd received from

God? As you look back, how did God end up working out his will despite your confusion? What did you learn?

6. Review Philip's discussion of his marriage on pages 223–25. God seeks not the clinging, helpless love of a child who has no real choice, Philip explains, but the mature, freely given commitment of a lover. This only comes about as the result of a faithful relationship with God—as we seek to please him, accept as our highest goal to know and love him, and make necessary sacrifices. In the end we *want* to please God.

   If you are married, have you found that commitment, faithfulness, and mutual sacrifice have made you a better person? Have they nurtured and grown the love you and your spouse have for each other? Have they been easy? If you are not married, do you have a friendship that has served in this manner, or have you seen a marriage that functioned this way?

   How do you see these same principles proving true for your relationship with God? Have commitment and sacrifice for God made you a better person? Have they put you in an attitude of heart and mind in which love for God could grow as a result?

7. Philip tells three stories to illustrate adult, not childish, motives for obedience (pp. 226–29). We desire to please Someone we respect, we feel gratitude for an extraordinary sacrifice, and we are reflecting our true identities as persons beloved by God. How much has God's love for you filled you with love for him? How much has God's love for you produced in you a love for others that has begun to direct your life?

   • I'm still stuck on trying to believe in God's love for me. It's very hard to manufacture love for God or anyone else when I don't fully sense his love for me.

- I believe in God's love with my mind, but that belief hasn't done much in my heart. I try to live the life of a Christian, but if I'm honest, I don't walk around with any great feeling of love for God or for others.
- God has been pretty persistent in showing me, in crazy but undeniable ways, that he loves me. It's still sinking in, but I'm finding that I'm softer inside toward him. I'm beginning to want what he wants more than what I want. And often I'm feeling compassion for other people, rather than criticism.
- It has changed my life to understand that God, as a loving parent, cares more than anything about my understanding and receiving his love for me. He cares more about this than about my following commands or being a particular kind of person. This realization has released in me a tender, trusting love for God and an unselfish love for other people.

Review 1 John 4:7–18. How important is a belief of the mind and heart in God's love for us? How does this belief affect our love for God and for others?

8. How much have basic spiritual disciplines such as daily prayer and Bible reading been a part of your life? How much do you know about, or have you experienced, other disciplines such as simplicity, solitude, submission, service, confession, worship, meditation, fasting, study, spiritual direction, Sabbath-keeping, and others?

If your answer to question 7 was similar to the first bullet point, what difference might it make to incorporate some spiritual disciplines into your life? How might some disciplines help you to know God's love for you?

If your answer to question 7 was similar to the second bullet point, can you identify any spiritual disciplines that might help you move your belief in God's love from your mind into your heart? Perhaps solitude, service, or journal-keeping?

Philip writes, "We live in a society that cannot comprehend those who fast or carve out two hours for a quiet time, and yet honors professional football players who work out with weights five hours a day and undergo a dozen knee and shoulder surgeries to repair the damage they inflict on themselves in the sport. Our aversion to spiritual discipline may reveal more about ourselves than about the 'saints' we criticize" (p. 231). What do you think about spiritual disciplines from this perspective? What roadblocks do you run into when you attempt to exercise spiritual disciplines?

9. "Love is what God wants from a relationship with us, but we humans tend to experience love like any emotion: intermittently, waxing and waning," Philip writes. "Discipline nurtures in us a spiritual staying power—the kind of love a couple enjoys on their golden anniversary, not at their wedding" (p. 231). Looking at your life with God in the past and considering your future with him, what kind of role do you think spiritual disciplines should play in your life? How might you go about incorporating some of these disciplines into your life?

Do you have any prayer needs to share with the group?

GRASPING FOR UNDERSTANDING OF MYSELF, MY GOD (10–20 MINUTES OR MORE)

Now we will look more deeply into our own lives and try to discern where we are in our stage of spiritual growth and where God might be prompting us to mature. Consider the following questions, answering true or false to each one.

- I have some strong opinions as to what Jesus' ideal for a Christian is. In a particular area (such as money, missions, social justice, the Holy Spirit, the end times, morality, or theology)—you might call it my "hot button"—I feel that mature Christians will see things the way I do.
- I believe Jesus' commands are important, but I also feel the freedom to focus on those commands which are relevant for me and not worry about those commands which don't seem necessary for me.
- I believe that if you have enough faith, God will grant you your heartfelt desires. Mature Christians see their hopes realized because of their unwavering faith.
- I believe that if I try to follow what God requires of me, I can expect God to keep the road ahead of me a smooth one. When I act rightly, God will make my life work out rightly.
- I'm angry with God about some issues he has not resolved in my life. I will trust him when he shows me I have reason to trust him.
- Some things in life never change, and I believe God expects us to accept that reality and not waste energy praying or hoping for change.
- God showers blessing and grace on those Christians who manage to get the Christian life right.
- Mature Christians have done enough study to understand God, the Bible, and the truths of life. They enter into faith because to them faith makes sense.
- I believe God reliably gives the mature Christian a clear vision of how he wants to use him or her.

How many statements above did you answer as true? Talk together as a group about those statements. Feel free to be honest, and search together for God's perspective. Know that we all have areas where growth and maturing is needed. Each statement above presents a distorted perspective on spiritual maturity. Where might God be urging you to grow?

CLINGING TO GOD DESPITE THE DISTANCE
(5 – 10 MINUTES)

We have talked about the importance of believing in God's love for us. When this belief becomes rooted in us, we instinctively love God and others in return. We have also discussed the importance of practicing regular disciplines in our life to keep us going when the feelings of love aren't so strong. Now we will pray about our need to know God's love and our need to keep going spiritually even when God's love or ours feels distant.

Close your eyes and ask God to help you where you need it. Do you need a true belief in God's love for you? Was this belief very real at one time, but the sense has faded within you? Does this belief seem real yet without the accompanying love for God or others in return? What disciplines might God be prompting you to use in your life to keep you attuned to him and responsive to him and others?

Focus your prayer in the area that fits your need. Pray for a receptive spirit to hear what God is saying to you. Perhaps the following words about God's love will help you focus your prayer.

> To believe means to realize not just with the head but also with the heart that God loves *me* in a creative, intimate, unique, reliable, and *tender* way. Creative: out of His love I came forth; through His love I am who I am. Intimate: His love reaches out to the deepest in me. Unique: His love embraces me as I am, not as I am considered to be by other people or supposed to be in my own self-image. Reliable: His love will never let me down. Tender . . . Tenderness is what happens to you when you know you are deeply and sincerely *liked* by someone.[1]

LONGING FOR GOD IN THE WEEK AHEAD
(OPTIONAL)

You can integrate this study into your life throughout the week by using the following suggestions and readings.

- If you would like to further explore the spiritual disciplines and the road to spiritual maturity, consider reading *Celebration of Discipline* by Richard Foster (HarperSanFrancisco, 1983), *The Spirit of the Disciplines* by Dallas Willard (HarperSanFrancisco, 1991), or

A Long Obedience in the Same Direction by Eugene Peterson (InterVarsity Press, 2000).

- Reflect on these Bible passages in the week ahead as your time allows.
  Day 1: 1 Corinthians 3:1–3
  Day 2: Psalm 131
  Day 3: 1 Corinthians 13:1–13
  Day 4: Ephesians 1:1–14
  Day 5: John 17:20–26

The following excerpt is from the book *The Spirit of the Disciplines* by Dallas Willard.

My central claim is that we *can* become like Christ by doing one thing—by following him in the overall style of life he chose for himself. If we have faith in Christ, we must believe that he knew how to live. We can, through faith and grace, become like Christ by practicing the types of activities he engaged in, by arranging our whole lives around the activities he himself practiced in order to remain constantly at home in the fellowship of his Father.

What activities did Jesus practice: Such things as solitude and silence, prayer, simple and sacrificial living, intense study and meditation upon God's Word and God's ways, and service to others. Some of these will certainly be even more necessary to us than they were to him, because of our greater or different need. . . .

Faith today is treated as something that only *should* make us different, not that actually *does* or *can* make us different. In reality we vainly struggle against the evils of this world, waiting to die and go to heaven. Somehow we've gotten the idea that the essence of faith is entirely a mental and inward thing.

I don't think anyone wanted or planned this state of affairs. We have simply let our thinking fall into the grip of a false opposition of grace to "works" that was caused by a mistaken association of works with "merit." And history has only made things worse. It has built a wall between faith and grace, and what we actually *do*. Of course we know there must be some connection between grace and life, but we can't seem to make it intelligible to ourselves. So, worst of all, we're unable to use that connection as the basis for specific guidance as to how to enter into Christ's character and power. . . .

I believe our present difficulty is one of misunderstanding how our experiences and actions enable us to receive the grace of God. There is a deep longing among Christians and non-Christians alike for the personal purity and power to live as our hearts tell us we should. What we need is a deeper insight into our practical relationship with God in redemption. We need an understanding that can guide us into constant interaction with the Kingdom of God as a real part of our daily lives, an *ongoing spiritual presence* that is at the same time a *psychological reality.* In other words, we must develop a psychologically sound theology of the spiritual life and of its disciplines to guide us. . . .

Holiness and devotion must now come forth from the closet and the chapel to possess the street and the factory, the schoolroom and boardroom, the scientific laboratory and the governmental office. Instead of a select few making religion their life, with the power and inspiration realized through the spiritual disciplines, all of us can make our daily lives and vocations be "the house of God and the gate of heaven." It can—and must—happen. And it will happen. The living Christ will make it happen through us as we dwell with him in life appropriately disciplined in the spiritual Kingdom of God.[2]

LIVING OUT
REDEMPTION

———— ⌒◇⌒ ————

The excerpt below is from *Reaching for the Invisible God*.

Just as we progress through the physical stages of child, adult, and parent, so do we also move through parallel stages in the spiritual life, though not in such a tidy sequence.

Every person has three great "cries from the heart," says Jean Vanier, who founded the l'Arche homes for the profoundly disabled. First, we cry to be loved by a father and mother who can hold us in our weakness. Each of us begins life as a helpless infant, and even in adulthood we never outgrow the need for parental love and comfort. That longing may ultimately turn us to God, as children in need of a heavenly Father.

Next, says Vanier, we feel an adult cry for a friend—someone with whom we can share our deepest secrets, whom we can trust without fear, whom we can love. That cry also may turn us to God, who surmounted the barrier of invisibility first by joining our species, then by promising to live inside us. "I no longer call you servants . . . but friends," Jesus said.

Finally, we have a cry to serve those weaker than ourselves. For many people, physical parenthood satisfies this need. Others—like Vanier the priest, like Jesus himself—seek out service to the poor, the lonely, the forgotten, the sick or disabled, in response to this cry from the heart.

Like any human parent, the mature Christian lives not for himself or herself, but for the sake of others. When I went through the New Testament marking Child, Adult, or Parent in the margin beside each appeal to goodness, I found many such passages directed to "parental" instincts. Gradually, gently, the writers press their readers to move beyond self-fulfillment.

The New Testament persistently presses us upward, toward higher motives for being good. A child wants to know what she can get away with; an adult understands that boundaries exist for his own good; a parent voluntarily sacrifices her freedom for the sake of others.

God knows we are but children, which is why the Bible so often draws on that human parallel. At the same time, God yearns for us to grow toward the Parent stage of sacrificial love, which most accurately reflects God's own nature. We draw near to God in likeness when we give ourselves away. In fact, as Jean Vanier insists, we *need* this further stage as an essential part of spiritual development; it teaches what we might otherwise never learn.

In a fundamental human paradox, the more a person reaches out beyond herself, the more she is enriched and deepened, and the more she grows in likeness to God. On the other hand, the more a person "incurves," to use Luther's word, the less human she becomes. Our need to give is as great as anyone's need to receive.

The parent stage represents an advanced state of maturity. Sooner or later, parents find themselves alone, facing stern trials without much guidance on how to proceed—a fact of life that applies to spiritual parents as well as physical. I have met Christians in difficult places such as Lebanon, Russia, and Somalia who were totally unprepared for this advanced state. They volunteered to serve others in a spirit of idealism. As trials increased, they anticipated a closer sense of God's presence, more support, stronger faith. Instead they found the opposite.

A friend of mine who researched thousands of saints in order to select 365 for a daily devotional guide told me that almost all of them climbed slopes of increasing difficulty. As God entrusts us with more responsibility, the hardships may increase as well. Feelings of abandonment intensify, any sense of the presence of God fades, and temptations and doubts multiply.

We need look no further than the Bible for examples of God's absence. "You have hidden your face from us," said Isaiah. "Why are you like a stranger in the land, like a traveler who stays only a night?"

demanded Jeremiah. Any relationship involves times of closeness and times of distance, and in a relationship with God, no matter how intimate, the pendulum will swing from one side to the other.

———— ✧ ————

Christians best influence the world by sacrificial love, the most effective way truly to change a world. Parents express love by staying up all night with sick children, working two jobs to pay school expenses, sacrificing their own desires for the sake of their children's. And every person who follows Jesus learns a similar pattern. God's kingdom gives itself away, in love, for that is precisely what God did for us.

Some college students strike out for the wilderness or take up meditation in order to "discover themselves." Jesus suggests that we discover that self not by staring inward but by gazing outward, not through introspection but through acts of love. No one can grasp how to be a parent by reading books before the birth of a child. You learn the role by doing a thousand mundane acts: calling the doctor during illness, preparing for the first day of school, playing catch in the backyard, consoling hurts and defusing tantrums. A spiritual parent goes through the same process. In the end, Jesus' prediction—"Whoever loses his life will preserve it"— proves true, for the downward surrender leads upward.

———— ✧ ————

The world is good. For this claim we have no less an authority than God himself. After each act of creation, Genesis 1 records the heartening refrain, "And God saw that it was good." His task finished, "God saw all that he had made, and it was very good."

From Augustine onward, Christian theology has insisted that what we call bad things are actually good things perverted. A lie warps truth; sexual immorality sullies the beauty of physical love; gluttony abuses food and drink. A parasite, evil must live off good, and has no ability to create anything new.

I have learned, though, to look beyond apparent negatives to the underlying good, starting with the human body. From Dr. Paul Brand, my coauthor on three books, I learned to "befriend" many bodily processes normally regarded as enemies. Virtually every activity of our body that we view with irritation or disgust—blister, callus, swelling, fever, sneeze, cough, vomiting, and especially pain—demonstrates the body's protective response. Without these warning signs and crucial steps in the healing process, we would live at great peril.

My emotional pains reveal an underlying good as well. What's good about fear? I try to imagine mountain climbing or downhill skiing without the safeguard of fear that keeps me from acting even more recklessly. Or I think of a world without loneliness, a form of pain that Adam felt even before the Fall. Would friendship and even love exist without the inbuilt sense of need, the prod that keeps us all from being hermits? We need the power of loneliness to nudge us toward other people.

Negative emotions can have positive value if responded to well. In the words of psychiatrist Gerald May, "In reality, our lack of fulfillment is the most precious gift we have. It is the source of our passion, our creativity, our search for God. All the best of life comes out of *our human yearning—our not being satisfied.*" We suffer most when we love most. We recoil from death because we want to keep on living.

I have learned an abiding appreciation for the goodness in this world, good that can be seen even in the residue of bad. When something bad happens—a disagreement with my wife, a painful misunderstanding with a friend, an ache of guilt over some responsibility I have let slide—I try to view it as I would view a physical pain, as a signal alerting me to attend to a matter that needs change. I strive to be grateful not for the pain itself but for the opportunity to respond, by mining good out of what looks bad.

The world is fallen. Adam and Eve gained the knowledge of good and evil by welcoming evil into the world, thus losing the chance to live as God intended. In our own times, technology repeats the cycle of Adam and Eve. We master the atom and nearly obliterate ourselves. We learn the secrets of life only to develop techniques to destroy the unborn and the aging. We unlock the genetic code and open a Pandora's box of ethics. We tame the Great Plains with agriculture and cause dust bowls, harvest rain forests and create floods, harness internal combustion and melt the icecaps. We link the world on an Internet only to find that the most downloaded items are pornographic. Every advance introduces yet another fall.

"And yet . . ."—those two words, according to Elie Wiesel, always apply—even in a badly fallen world we catch glimpses of the original goodness.

The world can be redeemed. Redemption promises not replacement— a wholly new creation imposed on the old—but a transformation that somehow makes use of all that went before. We will realize God's design as reclaimed originals, like a priceless oil painting restored after a fire or a cathedral rebuilt after a bombing. Redemption involves a kind of alchemy, a philosophers' stone that makes gold from clay. In the end, evil itself will serve as a tool of good.

The Christian story insists that history is, in lurches and detours, moving to a resolution. Every spark of beauty, worth, and meaning that we experience in this strange existence glimmers as a relic of a good world that still bears marks of its original design. Every twinge of pain, anxiety, cruelty, and injustice is a relic of the fall away from that design. And every demonstration of love, justice, peace, and compassion is a movement toward its ultimate redemption, the day when, in Paul's words, "the creation itself will be liberated from its bondage to decay and brought into the glorious freedom of the children of God."

ENCOUNTERING GOD THROUGH THOSE IN THE BIBLE (5 MINUTES)

Read the following Scripture passages.

Ephesians 1:3–14. Read this passage focusing on the redemption we have received through Jesus—we, who as sinners do not meet God's holy standards, were made holy when we accepted Jesus' death for us.

2 Corinthians 5:11–6:2. Read this passage focusing on our response to being redeemed. In love and gratitude for what God did for us through Christ, we in turn will act in love for others. Pay special attention to verses 19–20.

REACHING FOR GOD WITH OTHERS (25 MINUTES)

If you are in a large group, break into groups of four to six for this discussion time. Introduce yourselves to each other if necessary. Tell the others about a memorable childhood family vacation, when things didn't turn out as ideally as your parents had planned. Or tell of a vacation with your own children, when you wondered whether you'd have been better off staying home. In retrospect, were the vacations still worthwhile?

1. Philip writes of Jean Vanier's three cries from the heart: the cry to be loved by a father and mother who can hold us in our weakness; the cry for a friend whom we can share with, trust, and love; and the cry to serve those weaker than ourselves (p. 236). Usually these cries progress from one to the next, with all three cries still being active in adults. Was your cry for a parent to hold you in your weakness answered early in life? Or were your parents unable to adequately answer that cry? Do you find yourself still needing the love and support of your parents?

When did you begin to seek and find a true friend or friends whom you could share with, trust, and love? Or are you still trying to find a true friend?

When did you sense an inner desire to serve those weaker than yourself? Did this desire come after you had found your first two cries answered in large part?

Do you think a person typically progresses to this third cry if the first or second cries remain unanswered? Do parents have a hard time caring well for their children when their own first or second cries have not been adequately answered? Do humanitarian workers, pastors, church volunteers struggle to serve well or to find fulfillment when they have not received sufficient answers to their first two cries? Is there a difference between having a cry answered adequately and having a cry answered perfectly? Explain.

If either or both of a person's first two cries have not been answered, what hope is there? How might God help fill that void? Will such a person ever successfully move to the third cry?

2. Philip writes, "A child wants to know what she can get away with; an adult understands that boundaries exist for his own good; a parent voluntarily sacrifices her freedom for the sake of others" (p. 237). We live in a society in many ways foreign to these ideas. People flaunt their ability to sidestep the rules; boundaries are spoken of in the context of setting one's own; and freedoms are overwhelmingly defended rather than sacrificed. Do these societal norms indicate an immature society or simply a society in which alternate ways have been ingrained?

3. "Perhaps there is nothing in this world as powerful to break selfishness as is the simple act of looking at our own children," remarks Ronald Rolheiser. Review the rest of his quote on pages 237–38. If you are a parent, why is it that children break through our selfishness like nothing else can? What has being a parent revealed to you about how God feels toward you? If you are not a parent, share about a time when you served someone with a selfless love. What brought about the desire to do so?

Missionary-martyr Jim Elliot once observed that many Christians are so intent on doing something for God that they forget that God's main work is to make something of them. Parents, how have you found that your role as parent has changed you and helped you grow as a person? In what ways? And for everyone, when have you set out to do something for God and found that in the end what you did for God was much less significant than what God did in you through the process?

4. "The more a person 'incurves' [reaches inward without reaching out] . . . the less human she becomes," writes Philip. "Our need to give is as great as anyone's need to receive" (p. 239). Can you recall meeting anyone in your life who seemed an obvious target for the charity of others yet was compelled to serve others? Have you ever needed to serve despite your own neediness? Can this ever be unhealthy?

Review the story of Abbe Pierre on pages 239–40. Read it together if all have not done so. "No, no, it is you who have saved us," explained Abbe Pierre. "We must serve or we die." What did he mean? Why couldn't the beggars settle at last into a comfortable life and simply live as upstanding citizens of France? Was there a danger in staying at home and not feeling the need to cross a continent to help a stranger?

How does 2 Corinthians 5:11–6:2 speak to the above questions? Has God placed a need within us to care for others with his love? How is the Holy Spirit involved?

5. Speaking of saints, Philip writes that "almost all of them climbed slopes of increasing difficulty. As God entrusts us with more responsibility, the hardships may increase as well. Feelings of abandonment intensify, any sense of the presence of God fades, and temptations and doubts multiply" (p. 241). When and how have you met this sort of difficulty? At the time did you question God's goodness and his ability to guide? How did you make it through this time?

Henri Nouwen writes, "In the midst of pains and tribulations the first sign of the new life can be found and a joy can be experienced which is hidden in the midst of sadness" (p. 242). In your time of difficulty discussed above, did you experience new life in any way as a result of the hardship? Did you experience joy in the midst of sadness? Does the hope of new life and hidden joy change your perspective on a time of difficulty you are facing now?

6. Philip discusses his move to Colorado on pages 249–51. He found a paradise with blemishes. When have you had an experience of reveling in something good, only to find a dark side to it?

Philip explains that what we call bad things are actually good things perverted. And many apparent negatives have much underlying good. Psychiatrist Gerald May says, "In reality, our lack of fulfillment is the most precious gift we have. It is the source of our passion, our creativity, our search for God. All the best of life comes out of our human yearning—our not being satisfied." And Philip writes that when a bad thing happens, such as a disagreement, a misunderstanding, an ache of guilt, he tries to view it as a physical pain, a signal alerting him to attend to a matter that needs change. Do you look at your longings and upsets this way? Can you think of one personal longing or upset that is really a gift or a signal alerting you to the need for change?

Philip writes, "Redemption promises not replacement—a wholly new creation imposed on the old—but a transformation that somehow makes use of all that went before. We will realize God's design as reclaimed originals, like a priceless oil painting restored after a fire or a cathedral rebuilt after a bombing. Redemption involves a kind of alchemy, a philosophers' stone that makes gold from clay. In the end, evil itself will serve as a tool of good" (pp. 255–56).

How does Ephesians 1:3–14 support the ideas above? Which phrases speak of redemption and the transformation ahead of us?

Some Christians feel that this life on earth doesn't hold much significance in light of the eternity ahead for us. Does the idea of one day being a "reclaimed original" suggest that this life is important and closely connected to eternity? How do you feel about this life if it's true that one day you are to be transformed, keeping in some way all that went before, with the evil serving as a tool of the good? Does it make this life feel even more precious and significant? Does it give new importance to your relationship with God?

Do you have any prayer needs to share with the group?

GRASPING FOR UNDERSTANDING OF MYSELF, MY GOD (10–20 MINUTES OR MORE)

Now we will take time to look more closely at the three great cries of the heart identified by Jean Vanier. If you discussed the questions in the first part of the previous section, this exercise is best spent in personal thought, either now quietly with the group or during time set aside at home this week. Consider the following:

- Were your father and mother able for the most part to love you and hold you in your weakness throughout your childhood? Was one parent able and the other less able?
- If your parents are still alive, do they provide you with love and support now? Do you sense some kind of void within you because of this cry of the heart not being adequately answered in childhood or now?
- Do you have one or more friends with whom you can share deeply, whom you can trust without fear, and toward whom you can show love?
- If you have trouble sharing deeply, do you understand why? Do you feel self-conscious? Do you feel unworthy to be deeply known?
- If you cannot truly trust any friend, do you understand why? Is fear a controlling part of your life? Were you betrayed or abused by someone for whom you cared deeply? Has friendship been absent in your life for so long that you don't think of pursuing it anymore?
- If you have difficulty showing a caring, vulnerable love for any friend, do you understand why? Have you built walls inside to keep yourself from being vulnerable?
- Do any of these difficulties stem from your cry for the love of a parent not being answered?
- Do you serve anyone weaker than yourself, as a parent, a volunteer, a spiritual leader, a caring neighbor?
- If you don't have a desire to serve or don't find yourself able, is it because one or both of your first two cries of the heart have not been answered? See the paragraph with an asterisk at the bottom of page 244, in which Philip cautions that some Christians need a healing emphasis on self-possession before they can think about self-sacrifice.
- What needs to happen if one, two, or three of your cries of the heart are not being adequately answered? Would professional

counseling help? Pastoral counseling? Honesty and prayer with a friend? Do you need to work on being honest with yourself about your unmet needs?

- Do you believe God can enter into the void in you and meet your needs directly and through other people?

Spend time in prayer, telling God about the cries of your heart. Tell him your needs. Ask him to help you, to meet you where you feel a void, to change you where necessary, and to bring others to help answer your cry.

CLINGING TO GOD DESPITE THE DISTANCE
(5 – 10 MINUTES)

We talked toward the end of today's discussion about viewing personal longings as a gift and upsets as a signal alerting us to the need for change. Now we will spend silent time together in prayer, asking God to create in us an understanding that will cause us to respond to longings and upsets in this way.

As you pray, first present one of your longings to God. Maybe your longing to get married, to find a fulfilling job, to have a child, to find healing for a relationship. Tell God of this longing and ask him to help you understand the gift that resides in your longing. Maybe your longing keeps you reaching out to others or connecting with God or searching deeply within yourself or living in humility and compassion for others. Ask God to give you thankfulness for the good things your longing is producing in you.

Next present a recent upset to God. Maybe a recent argument with a family member or friend, an insult you have received, inattention from someone important to you, guilt over something you did or did not do. Tell God about what has bothered you, and ask him to help you understand your feelings as a signal alerting you to the need for change in yourself or in a relationship. Ask for understanding about the change that is needed and for help in making the change.

LONGING FOR GOD IN THE WEEK AHEAD
(OPTIONAL)

You can integrate this study into your life throughout the week by using the following suggestions and readings.

- This week pay special attention to your longings and your feelings of upset. Ponder and pray about the deeper good that is a part of these feelings.
- As you read the book of James this week, focus on what James is saying about the reason we do good works—in response to our redemption. Focus also on what James says about the underlying motives for the things we do. As James points out, our problems and negative emotions can bring about good or destruction.

  Day 1: James 1
  Day 2: James 2
  Day 3: James 3
  Day 4: James 4
  Day 5: James 5

The following reading is excerpted from *The Living Reminder* by Henri Nouwen.

The French writer-politician Andre Malraux writes in his *Anti-Memoirs*, "One day it will be realized that men are distinguishable from one another as much by the forms their memories take as by their characters." This is a very important observation. The older we grow the more we have to remember, and at some point we realize that most, if not all, of what we have is memory. Our memory plays a central role in our sense of being. Our pains and joys, our feelings of grief and satisfaction, are not simply dependent on the events of our lives, but also, and even more so, on the ways we remember these events. The events of our lives are probably less important than the form they take in the totality of our story. Different people remember a similar illness, accident, success, or surprise in very different ways, and much of their sense of self derives less from what happened than from how they remember what happened, how they have placed the past events into their own personal history.

It is not surprising, therefore, that most of our human emotions are closely related to our memory. Remorse is a biting memory, guilt is an accusing memory, gratitude is a joyful memory, and all such emotions are deeply influenced by the way we have integrated past events into our way of being in the world. In fact, we perceive our world with our memories. Our memories help us to see and understand new impressions and give them a place in our richly varied life experiences. . . .

It is no exaggeration to say that the suffering we most frequently encounter in the ministry is a suffering of memories. They are the wounding memories that ask for healing. Feelings of alienation, loneliness, separation; feelings of anxiety, fear, suspicion, and related symptoms such as nervousness, sleeplessness, nail-biting—these are all part of the forms which certain memories have taken. These memories wound because they are often deeply hidden in the center of our being and very hard to reach. While the good memories may be present to us in outer signs such as trophies, decorations, diplomas, precious stones, vases, rings, and portraits, painful memories tend to remain hidden from us in the corner of our forgetfulness. It is from this hidden place that they escape healing and cause so much harm.

Our first and most spontaneous response to our undesirable memories is to forget them. When something painful has happened, we quickly say to ourselves and to each other: "Let's forget it, let's act as if it did not happen, let's not talk about it, let's think about happier things." We want to forget the pains of the past—our personal, communal, and national traumas—and live as if they did not really happen. But by not remembering them, we allow the forgotten memories to become independent forces that can exert a crippling effect on our functioning as human beings. When this happens we become strangers to ourselves because we cut down our own history to a pleasant, comfortable size and try to make it conform to our own daydreams. Forgetting the past is like turning our most intimate teacher against us. By refusing to face our painful memories, we miss the opportunity to change our hearts and grow mature in repentance. When Jesus says, "It is not the healthy who need the doctor, but the sick" (Mark 2:17), he affirms that only those who face their wounded condition can be available for healing and so enter into a new way of living.[1]

BAD TURNED GOOD

The excerpt below is from *Reaching for the Invisible God*.

The world is good. The world is fallen. The world can be redeemed. If this sequence describes the story of the universe, then I must learn to look at the world, and myself, through that lens. Faith means developing an ability to accept that point of view, which I will never fully grasp until I reach heaven, no matter how things look here on earth. I learn to trust that God's mysterious style of working on this planet, and of relating to us his creatures, will one day fit into a pattern that makes sense.

Philosopher Nicholas Rescher likens communicating with God to talking over an old-fashioned telephone system. Other conversations bleed in, static drowns out the voice, the line breaks abruptly—and still we call out, "Hello! Hello! Are you there?" According to the apostle Paul, though, these difficulties in knowing God are a temporary condition: "Now we see but a poor reflection as in a mirror; then we shall see face to face. Now I know in part; then I shall know fully, even as I am fully known." When God finally restores creation to its original design, any gulf between visible and invisible worlds will disappear. The goal of history, a goal God has staked his existence on, is to bring the two worlds together once more, to reconcile them.

Beginning with the first chapters of Genesis and ending with the last chapters of Revelation, I detect two main power streams in the history of this planet. First, evil seizes what is good and despoils it. Since the

Fall we have lived in a world dominated by powers that are not morally neutral but rather tilted toward evil, as any history book or daily newspaper makes evident. Violence and injustice should not surprise us for we belong to an age in which evil rules.

In opposition, God unleashes a stream of power to redeem what evil has spoiled. For now, God has chosen to exercise his power through the most unlikely foot soldiers: flawed human beings. Because of these tactics, it may sometimes appear that God is losing the battle. The final victory will be won only when, in power and glory, God ends forever the reign of evil.

The day will come, I believe, when one set of powers vanquishes the other; we have Jesus' resurrection as a bright promise of that day. Until then, I experience these conflicting power streams every day, all day long. The powers work subtly, invisibly, and always I find myself caught in the two great power streams of history, one defacing the good and the other seeking to redeem what has been despoiled.

———— ⌘ ————

I think of God's style as "ironic." A more straightforward approach would respond to each new problem with an immediate solution. A woman gets sick; God heals her. A man is falsely imprisoned; God releases him. Rarely does God use such an approach, however. An author of great subtlety, he lets the plot line play out in perilous ways, then ingeniously incorporates those apparent detours into the route home.

It should not surprise us that a sovereign God uses bad things as the raw material for fashioning good. The symbol of our faith, after all, which we now stamp in gold and wear around our necks or chisel in stone and place atop our churches, is a replica of a Roman execution device. God did not save Jesus from the cross but "ironically" saved others through Jesus' death on the cross. In the Incarnation, God's power stream of redeeming good from evil was stealthily underway. God overcomes evil with good, hate with love, and death with resurrection.

As my faith grows, so does my confidence that my individual life is contributing in some small way to a larger story. My own story contains details that I regret and may even resent: pain from childhood, illness and injury, times of poverty, wrong choices, broken relationships, missed opportunities, disappointment in my own failures. Can I trust, truly trust, that God can weave these redemptively into my overall story, as "unwilling instruments of grace"?

God grants us freedom to rebel against the original design of creation, yet even as we do so we end up "ironically" serving his eventual goal of restoration. If I accept that blueprint—a huge step of faith, I confess—it transforms how I view both good and bad things that happen. Good things, such as health, talent, and money, I can present to God as offerings for his use. And bad things too—disability, poverty, family dysfunction, failures—can be "redeemed" as the very instruments that drive me to God.

I have kept circling around the age-old question of "Why do bad things happen, even to good people?" because this issue more than any other introduces confusion, and even a sense of betrayal, into a relationship with God. How can we trust in a loving God who allows such bad things to happen? Are the many terrible things that happen on earth God's will? Why must God use an "ironic" style—why not just prevent tragedy in the first place?

The British bishop Leslie Weatherhead makes helpful distinctions in the phrase "the will of God." A sovereign God interacting with a free creation involves at least three kinds of "wills," he says. First, there is God's intentional will. We know what God intends, for the first two chapters of Genesis spell out a world of perfect goodness, and Revelation ends with a similar landscape.

The Fall, however, changed the rules of the planet. In the wake of a decisive victory by the power stream of evil, many bad things appeared on earth. God must then have a "circumstantial will" that adapts to the evil conditions of earth. Its original goodness having been spoiled on this planet, God must instead salvage good from bad.

God's plan moves forward despite the evil circumstances, albeit in very different ways. This last pattern Weatherhead calls God's "ultimate will." To those who trust him, God promises to use any circumstances to serve his ultimate will. God previewed in his own Son the ultimate triumph of his ironic style of redemption.

On this planet, for this time, God allows us to be put in harm's way. Buildings collapse, tectonic plates shift, viruses proliferate, evil people resort to violence. From what we know about the character of God, none of these things reflect his intentional will. Nor, if we believe God's promises, do they reflect his ultimate will. In the meantime, though, the time in which we spend all our days on planet earth, bad things will inevitably happen.

———— ✧ ————

Listen to any pop music station or watch MTV and try to find a song that does *not* feature the theme of romantic love. Remarkably, most marriages worldwide conjoin men and women who have never felt a twinge of romantic love and may not recognize the sensation if it hit them. Teenagers in much of Africa and Asia take for granted the reality of marriages arranged by their parents in the same way we take for granted romantic love.

In fact, societies that practice arranged marriages tend to have much lower divorce rates than those that emphasize adolescent love. I doubt seriously that the West will ever abandon the notion of romantic love, no matter how poorly it serves as a basis for family stability. But through my conversations with Christians from different cultures I have begun to see how an arranged marriage might serve as a helpful model in relating to God.

In the U.S. and other Western-style cultures, people tend to marry because they are attracted to another's appealing qualities: a fresh smile, wittiness, a pleasing figure, athletic ability, charm. Over time these qualities may change, with the physical attributes, especially, deteriorating with age. Meanwhile, unexpected surprises will surface—slatternly housekeeping, bouts of depression, dissimilar sexual appetites—which disrupt the romance. In contrast, the partners in an arranged marriage do not center their relationship around mutual attractions. After your parents' decision, you accept that you will live for many years with someone you now barely know. The overriding question changes from "Whom should I marry?" to "Given this partner, what kind of marriage can we construct together?"

A similar pattern applies in a relationship with God. I have no control over God's qualities, such as his invisibility. God is free, with a "personality" and features that exist whether I like them or not. I have no choice about many of the details of my own makeup either. Taking the Western romantic approach, I can resent this quality or that one of God's and wish he ran the world differently. I can demand that God change my circumstances before I trust him with my life. Or I can take a very different approach. I can humbly accept God as he is revealed in Jesus and also accept myself, flaws and all, as the person God has chosen. I do not go in with a list of demands that must be met before I take the vow. Like a spouse in an arranged marriage, I pre-commit to God regardless.

BAD TURNED GOOD

Faith means taking a vow "for better or for worse, for richer or for poorer, in sickness and in health," to love God and cling to him no matter what. That involves risk, of course, for I may discover that what God asks of me conflicts with my selfish desires. Happily, the spirit of arranged marriage works two ways: God also pre-commits to me, promising a future and eternal life that will redeem the circumstances I now struggle with. God does not accept me conditionally, on the basis of my performance, but bestows his love and forgiveness freely, despite my innumerable failures.

Every human marriage has crisis times, moments of truth when one partner (or both) is tempted to give up. Older married couples will admit that during these times they questioned the entire relationship. Now, though, they retell the stories with humor and even nostalgia, for the crises fit together into—indeed, they helped form—a pattern of love and trust. Looking back from the vantage point of a few decades, it seems clear that the couple's mutual response to stormy times was what gave their marriage its enduring strength. A relationship with God can work the same way.

———

Indeed, in an odd sort of way, human beings need problems more than we need solutions. Problems stretch us and press us toward dependence on God. As the Bible reiterates, success represents a far greater danger. Samson, Saul, Solomon, and scores of others show that success leads toward pride and self-satisfaction, a path away from dependence and often a prelude to a fall.

God does not promise to solve all our problems, at least not in the manner we want them to be solved. (I find no characters in the Bible who lived a problem-free existence.) Rather, God calls us to trust him and to obey—whether we live in affluence and success or whether, like some Christians, we spend our days in a concentration camp. What matters most to God is what we create from the raw material.

In this hard task we have the pattern of Jesus himself who, when he came to earth, could have chosen any set of "raw materials" and deliberately settled on poverty, family shame, suffering, and rejection. He did not exempt himself from the annoyances of life on this planet, as if to prove that none of these circumstances need cancel out a healthy relationship with the Father. Perhaps we should say "Christ is the pattern" rather than "Christ is the answer," because Jesus' own life did not offer the answers most people are looking for. Not once did he use supernatural powers to improve his family, protect himself from harm, or increase his comfort and wealth.

———— ⌘ ————

"It is not up to you to finish the work, but neither are you free not to take it up," goes an old Talmudic saying. The work is God's work, the work of reclaiming and redeeming a planet badly damaged. For the Jew and Christian both, that work means bringing a touch of peace, justice, hope, healing, *shalom* wherever our hands touch. For the Christian it means doing so as a follower of Jesus, who made possible the redemption we could never accomplish on our own.

ENCOUNTERING GOD THROUGH THOSE IN THE BIBLE (10 MINUTES)

Read the following Scripture passages in the order in which they appear.
   Mark 15:16–37
   Philippians 2:5–11
   1 Corinthians 1:26–31
   Romans 8:28–37

REACHING FOR GOD WITH OTHERS (25 MINUTES)

If you are in a large group, break into groups of four to six for this discussion time. Introduce yourselves to each other if necessary. Tell the others about one of the most beautiful places in which you have ever hiked (or walked or driven, if you are not a hiker).

1. Philip uses the analogy of a climb to the top of a summit to illustrate the faith Christians must hold to in our journey on earth as we await heaven. "Only when I reach the summit does the entire landscape fit together. . . . I learn to trust that God's mysterious style of working on this planet, and of relating to us his creatures, will one day fit into a pattern that makes sense" (pp. 259–60). How much of this kind of faith do you have at this stage in your life?
   • I haven't had a lot of trouble understanding God's ways. In fact, I feel offended when people talk of God not making sense. The problem is with people, not with God.

———————

- I'm barely climbing now. I honestly don't know if I'll reach the summit. Heaven is the furthest thing from my mind, and I don't see how my life can ever make sense.
- I have climbed so steadily for so long. . . . I've always believed what Yancey says, but lately I've been losing steam. I don't know what's wrong—my faith has faded.
- I've had a glimpse in my life of what Yancey means. A few of my trials have worked to bring some unexpected good. Those glimpses keep me going and keep me believing.
- This kind of faith is the only thing that keeps me going. I couldn't endure life without it. Even when God himself feels distant, this hope keeps me from giving up.

Thinking back on the passage from Mark you have just read, how do you think the disciples felt after Jesus' crucifixion? How would they have answered the above question? Did they have any idea how Jesus' execution would fit into God's promise of a reigning King? Is Jesus' story of suffering on earth similar to your own story in any way? (The Bible tells us that we Christians will suffer as Jesus did.)

Do you believe that one day every knee will bow at the name of Jesus, as Philippians 2:10 says? If that day is imminent, how can we let it make a difference in our present lives, in view of the future that is ahead for us?

2. Read the quote by Teilhard de Chardin on page 262. Can you share with the group about an unavoidable difficulty in your life, or a personal fault, that God has transfigured into a good plan for your life?

   In what way can you affirm Paul's words in 1 Corinthians 1:26–31? How has God worked through you despite your lack of wisdom and influence?

3. Turn to page 265, where Philip discusses Bishop Leslie Weatherhead's explanation of the three kinds of wills of God. God's intentional will gives way to his circumstantial will when perfect goodness in our life is ruined by the influence of sin or evil. Taking circumstances as they are, God salvages good from the bad. Is this distinction helpful or just confusing? Consider a past heartache or trial. What was God's intentional will in your situation? Can you see now what his circumstantial will has brought about in your life to redeem the evil?

   Consider a current heartache or trial. What was God's intentional will in your situation? Can you see yet, or speculate on, how his circumstantial will is going to redeem the good gone awry?

   What is God's ultimate will for you and your life?

What does Romans 8:28–37 say about God's ultimate will for you? How does this truth make a difference in how you feel about the difficulties you are facing now?

Philip writes, "In the face of tragedy, I can respond either by blaming and turning against God or by turning toward him, trusting him to fashion good out of bad . . . [making my story] in some ways even richer, redeemed" (p. 267). If you are honest, which way do you usually respond to God? If you respond the first way, do you see any hope for changing your response to one more like the second? If you respond the second way, or strive to, how have you become able to make this response?

4. Review Philip's comparison of a relationship with God to an arranged marriage (pp. 269–72). Just as with an arranged spouse, I have no control over God's qualities, such as his invisibility. I can take the Western romantic approach and resent this or that quality of God's and wish he ran the world differently or demand he change my circumstances. Or, as with an arranged spouse, I can humbly accept God as he is revealed in Jesus and also accept myself, flaws and all, as the person God has chosen.

Many explanations can be given for the breakup of a marriage in the West. Similar explanations might be given for a break with God. Consider the following. Have you ever had any of these feelings? Do you have any of them now?

- I've had doubts about God since the beginning. It's not ever going to work. I may have committed myself to him at one time, but I don't know if I can play this game anymore.
- I thought I knew God. I had every reason to expect certain things that I feel are basic to a relationship with him. Boy, did I have it wrong. God hasn't come through in many of the ways I expected.

- Things were great in the beginning between God and me. But I'm not the same person anymore. I've grown in ways that make me feel differently about him, and I think he's grown away from me too.
- God was wonderful at first. But after I'd been a Christian for a while, our relationship really changed. The things I loved about our relationship ended, and I feel I don't even know him now.
- We were close for quite a while, but life has gradually grown busier and I've had a lot taking up my time and attention. It's probably more my fault than God's, yet I don't know if we can ever recapture what we've lost.

Now look at your relationship with God from the perspective of an arranged marriage. How would you respond to the feelings you've chosen from the above list if you viewed your relationship with God as an arranged marriage?

See the quote by G. K. Chesterton on page 269. How do these words speak to your spiritual struggle? Can anyone in the group share about how Chesterton's words have proven true in your own marriage? Can anyone tell about how his words have proven true in your relationship with God?

5. Review Dorothy Sayers' analogy of an artist on page 272. "Indeed, in an odd sort of way, human beings need problems more than we need solutions," writes Philip. "Problems stretch us and press us toward dependence on God." Can you think of one problem or lim-

itation in your life which has clearly increased your dependence on God and resulted in a stronger faith?

What kind of limitations and problems did Jesus deal with while on earth? Did his advantages as the Son of God mean he encountered no difficulties in his relationship with God? Why or why not? Does Jesus identify with your limitations and problems in any way because of the life he lived? See the last paragraph on page 273.

6. Philip writes, "God's goodness does not mean we will not get hurt, not in this fallen world at least. His goodness goes deeper than pleasure and pain, somehow incorporating both. . . . Some pains, whether the precisely-shaped pain of loss or the formless pain of unfulfilled longing, never go away. The wound will never heal completely, the problem never find a pure solution. We are offered instead the less satisfying but more realistic hope that God can redeem even the wound" (pp. 274–76).

Do you agree with Philip that some wounds will never heal completely here on earth? Whether or not you agree, how do you feel about the possibility that your wound will never heal completely here on earth? Strangely relieved because you can accept the lingering pain and move on? Deeply troubled that God can't manage to heal you completely? Does it make a difference to you that despite the lingering pain, God can redeem the wound? What might that look like for you?

7. An old Talmudic saying goes, "It is not up to you to finish the work, but neither are you free not to take it up." We are a part of God's process of redemption through Jesus. In what way is God using you in his process? How does this saying speak to you about your role in this piece of redemption?

Do you have any prayer needs to share with the group?

GRASPING FOR UNDERSTANDING OF MYSELF, MY GOD (10–20 MINUTES OR MORE)

Now we will look deeper into ourselves to better understand our personal level of faith. Begin this exercise with your small group if time permits. Continue to consider the questions in your own personal time. We'll focus on Philip's following words:

> Only when I reach the summit does the entire landscape fit together.... Faith means developing the ability to accept that [the world is good, fallen, and can be redeemed], which I will never fully grasp until I reach the summit, no matter how things look along the trail. I learn to trust that God's mysterious style of working on this planet, and of relating to us his creatures, will one day fit into a pattern that makes sense.

1. Do you live out of a deep belief that the world is good because it was made by a good Creator, the world is fallen because of sin, and the world can be redeemed because of the everlasting sacrifice of God's Son, Jesus? Consider these words by Dallas Willard regarding belief.

> Remember, to believe something is to act as if it is so. To believe that two plus two equals four is to behave accordingly when trying to find out how many apples or dollars are in the house. The advantage of believing it is not that we can pass tests in arithmetic; it is that we can deal much more successfully with reality.[1]

Does your belief cause you to act as if you believe your life will one day make sense even if it does not seem to make sense now? Does your belief cause you to act as if your relationship with God will one day be good and perfect and completely satisfying even if it does not always seem so now? What are some ways in which your actions would prove your belief?

Do any of the following describe you?

- I have a hard time really believing the world is good. I tend to look at most everything and everyone with a skeptic's eye, focusing only on the tainted aspects of this world. This makes my belief in redemption pretty shaky.
- I have a hard time really believing the world is fallen. People may make mistakes and the earth may experience challenges, but I'm an eternal optimist. I insist on seeing the good and believing that all our efforts for positive change will be successful.
- I have a hard time believing we'll come full circle, with the fallen redeemed and the good restored. I tend to feel more that we had our chance and we blew it, and now we will live forever with the consequences.

2. If any of the above bulleted viewpoints describe you, you might consider focusing on how these principles apply in Jesus' life. Would it help you to focus over a period of time on the goodness Jesus demonstrated, the fallenness that caused his suffering, or the redemption he guaranteed through his resurrection? Would meditation and prayer help you to accept belief in all three realities and integrate this belief into your actions?

CLINGING TO GOD DESPITE THE DISTANCE
(5–10 MINUTES)

Now we will spend some time in silent prayer. Instead of opening your hands to God, as we have done before, cup your hands, resting them in your lap. Imagine you are holding in your cupped hands a pain that has been ongoing for some time—an unfulfilled longing, a loss that hurt you deeply, a relational wound that has never healed, an illness with a potentially threatening prognosis.

Sit with God and the pain you hold, and talk with God about the possibility that this pain may never heal completely here on earth. Ask

God to help you live with this reality, even as you trust him to bring any level of healing he chooses.

Then commit your pain to God for the redemption he promises. Ask him to bring good in you and in your life through this pain you carry.

LONGING FOR GOD IN THE WEEK AHEAD (OPTIONAL)

You can integrate this study into your life throughout the week by using the following suggestions and readings.

- This week live in awareness of the presence of redemption in the here and now. What hints can you find in your life that God even now is redeeming a deep pain or struggle?
- As you read the Beatitudes and the Sermon on the Mount this week, consider how the sequence of goodness, fallenness, and redemption inspires Jesus' sometimes paradoxical teaching ("Blessed are the poor"—an example of God's redemption; "Give to the one who asks you"—an example of God's desire for goodness to be felt by all).
  Day 1: Matthew 5:1–20
  Day 2: Matthew 5:21–48
  Day 3: Matthew 6:1–15
  Day 4: Matthew 6:16–34
  Day 5: Matthew 7:1–28

The following reading is excerpted and adapted from *The Jesus I Never Knew* by Philip Yancey.

The Sermon on the Mount haunted my adolescence. I would read a book like Charles Sheldon's *In His Steps*, solemnly vow to act "as Jesus would act," and turn to Matthew 5–7 for guidance. What to make of such advice? Should I offer myself to be pummeled by the motorcycle-riding "hoods" in school? Tear out my tongue after speaking a harsh word to my brother?

Now that I am an adult, the crisis of the Sermon on the Mount still has not gone away. Though I have tried at times to dismiss it as rhetorical excess, the more I study Jesus, the more I realize that the statements contained here lie at the heart of his message. *If I fail to understand his teaching, I fail to understand him.*

To put the issue bluntly, are the Beatitudes true? If so, why doesn't the church encourage poverty and mourning and meekness and persecution instead of striving against them? What is the real meaning of the Beatitudes, this mysterious ethical core of Jesus' teaching?

I am not, and may never be, ready to declare, "This is what the Beatitudes mean." But gradually, I have come to recognize them as important truths. To me they apply on at least three levels.

Dangled Promises. The Beatitudes are not merely Jesus' nice words of consolation to the unfortunates. Unlike medieval kings who threw coins to the masses (or modern politicians who make promises to the poor just before elections), Jesus had the ability to offer his audience lasting, even eternal rewards. Alone of all people on earth, Jesus had actually lived "on the other side," and he who came down from heaven knew well that the spoils of the kingdom of heaven can easily counterbalance whatever misery we might encounter in this life. Those who mourn *will be comforted;* the meek *will inherit the earth;* the hungry *will be filled;* the pure *will see God.* Jesus could make such promises with authority, for he had come to establish God's kingdom that would rule forever.

The Great Reversal. I have also come to believe that the Beatitudes describe the present as well as the future. They neatly contrast how to succeed in the kingdom of heaven as opposed to the kingdom of this world. The Beatitudes express quite plainly that God views the world through a different set of lenses. God seems to prefer the poor and those who mourn to the Fortune 500 and supermodels who frolic on the beach. Oddly, God may prefer South Central L.A. to Malibu Beach, and Rwanda to Monte Carlo. In fact, one could almost subtitle the Sermon on the Mount not "survival of the fittest" but "triumph of the victims." With nowhere else to turn, the desperate just may turn to Jesus, the only one who can offer the deliverance they long for.

Psychological Reality. The Beatitudes reveal that what succeeds in the kingdom of heaven also benefits us most in this life here and now. I would rather spend time among the servants of this world than among the stars: they possess qualities of depth and richness and even joy that I have not found elsewhere. The servants clearly emerge as the favored ones, the graced ones. Somehow in the process of losing their lives, they find them.

When I first heard the Beatitudes, they sounded to me like impossible ideals given by some dreamy mystic. Now, though, I see them as truths proclaimed by a realist. Jesus knew how life works, in the kingdom of heaven as well as the kingdom of this world. In a life characterized by poverty, mourning, meekness, a hunger for righteousness, mercy, purity, peacemaking, and persecution, Jesus himself embodied the Beatitudes. Perhaps he even conceived the Beatitudes as a sermon to himself as well as to the rest of us, for he would have much opportunity to practice these hard truths.[2]

CHAPTER 23

HOPE TO
HOLD ON TO

———— ◦\◦ ————

The excerpt below is from *Reaching for the Invisible God*.

Early in this book I told of a friend who said to me, "I have no trouble believing God is good. My question is, more, What good is he? I cry out to God for help, and it's hard to know just how he answers. Really, what can we count on God for?" That question has lurked in the background of every chapter and is my true motivation in writing the book. In all other personal relationships we have some idea what to expect and count on. What about with God?

I find at least the hint of an answer in a phrase from Dallas Willard, whose book *The Divine Conspiracy* includes these words tucked away in a subordinate clause: "Nothing irredeemable has happened to us or can happen to us on our way to our destiny in God's full world." The world is good, the world is fallen, the world can be redeemed—in effect, Willard affirms that this same plot applies not only to the universe as a whole but to every one of God's followers. Nothing we encounter lies beyond the range of God's redemptive power.

———— ◦\◦ ————

Every person on earth lives out a unique script of hardship: singleness when marriage was always a goal, or a physical disability, or poverty, childhood abuse, racial prejudice, chronic illness, family dysfunction, addiction, divorce. If I envision God as Zeus-like, aiming thunderbolts on the wretched humans below, then naturally I will direct my anger and frustration at God, the immediate cause of my hardship. If, on the other hand, I perceive God as working from below, under the surface, calling out to us through each weakness and limitation, I open the possibility of redemption for the very thing I resent most about my life.

Paul Tournier, a medical doctor and counselor, wrote the book *Creative Suffering* in order to explore a phenomenon that had always puzzled him: The most successful people are often the products of difficult and unhappy families. A colleague investigating leaders with the greatest influence on world history had discovered that almost all—his list of three hundred included Alexander the Great, Julius Caesar, Louis XIV, George Washington, Napoleon, and Queen Victoria—had one thing in common: they were orphans. It baffled Tournier that whereas he spent his time lecturing on the importance of a mother and father cooperating to produce a nourishing family environment, these leaders all emerged from a state of emotional deprivation. An orphan himself, Tournier began to look at hardship as something not simply to be eliminated, but rather harnessed for redemptive good. Although we have no right to impose cheery formulas of redemptive suffering on others, neither can we ignore witnesses who insist on that truth.

———— ✿ ————

I have an unmarried friend who prays earnestly for God to lessen or even remove his sexual drive. It causes him constant temptation, he says. Pornography distracts him, plunges him into a failure spiral, and ruins his devotional life. As gently as I can, I tell him that I doubt God will answer the prayer as he wants, by recalibrating his testosterone level. More likely, he will learn fidelity the way anyone learns it, relying on discipline, community, and constant pleas of dependence.

For whatever reason, God has let this broken world endure in its fallen state for a very long time. For those of us who live in that broken world, God seems to value character more than our comfort, often using the very elements that cause us most discomfort as his tools in fashioning that character. A story is being written, with an ending only faintly glimpsed by us. We face the choice of trusting the Author along the way or striking out alone. Always, we have the choice.

In my own spiritual life, I am trying to remain open to new realities, not blaming God when my expectations go unmet but trusting him to lead me through failures toward renewal and growth. I am also seeking a trust that "the Father knows best" in how this world is run. Reflecting on Old Testament times, I see that the more overt way in which I may want God to act does not achieve the results I might expect. And when God sent his own Son—sinless, non-coercive, full of grace and healing—we killed him. God himself allows what he does not prefer, in order to achieve some greater goal.

O felix culpa, or "Oh, happy guilt," was a staple of medieval theology, one still celebrated in the Holy Saturday liturgy. It means, simply, that in a mysterious way we are better off now than before Adam's "Fortunate Fall." The final chapter of the story, redemption, achieves a state superior to the first chapter, creation. As Augustine expressed it, "God judged it better to bring good out of evil than to suffer no evil at all." The final result will prove worth the cost.

Surely we are better off in at least one way: we have Jesus, who in his life and death accomplished for the entire cosmos the same story of redemption promised to each of us individually. I have focused on a relationship with God from the human point of view, the only point of view I have. Yet I am aware that just as we must make adjustments to "know God personally"—a God invisible and utterly unlike us—so God must make adjustments in order to know us. Indeed, God had to subject himself to the very same plot. The early Christian writers spoke of Jesus as the "recapitulation" of the human drama.

The world is good. God pronounced it as such after each day's creative work. Even in its fallen state, God judged the world—judged us— worth the rescue effort, worth the condescension to the bounds of time and space, worth dying for.

The world is fallen. God has promised to abolish suffering, poverty, evil, and death. His means of doing so, however, involved absorbing those very things in strong doses. Though God may not prevent the hardships of this free and dangerous world, neither did God seek personal immunity from them. Deliberately, God's Son Jesus submitted to the worst of this fallen world.

Finally, *the world can be redeemed.* That was the whole point in Jesus' coming to earth. In the height of irony, God transformed ultimate evil into ultimate good, working through humanity's violence and hatred to accomplish our redemption. As Paul expressed it, "And having disarmed the powers and authorities, he made a public spectacle of them, triumphing over them *by the cross.*"

History changed forever as a result of Jesus' time on earth. And God's overall plan for the universe will ultimately prevail; history merely fills in the details. Today, we refer to the day Jesus died as Good Friday, not "Dark Friday" or "Tragic Friday." It is by his stripes, after all, that we are healed.

ENCOUNTERING GOD THROUGH THOSE IN THE BIBLE (3 MINUTES)

Read together John 14:1–6.

REACHING FOR GOD WITH OTHERS (25 MINUTES)

If you are in a large group, break into groups of four to six for this discussion time. Introduce yourselves to each other if necessary. Can anyone in the group tell of a time when you were part of an underdog team that pulled off an amazing victory, or a time when you were chosen for an honor or a position no one would have expected?

1. Philip writes, "Every person on earth lives out a unique script of hardship: singleness when marriage was always a goal, or a physical disability, or poverty, childhood abuse, racial prejudice, chronic illness, family dysfunction, addiction, divorce" (p. 280). He goes on to discuss people like George Washington, Napoleon, and Queen Victoria, who were orphans, and others like Mother Teresa, Alexander Solzhenitsyn, and Nelson Mandela, who grew up under difficult conditions. All became influential leaders who continue to impact our world today. They are just a few examples of redemptive suffering.

   Can you think of one person you know who has faced serious difficulty and allowed the work of redemption to bring about significant good?

If God were to use your suffering for some kind of significant good, would you feel that the suffering was worthwhile? Do you think this sort of redemption erases the pain? Might redemption transform the pain in some way so it has only a secondary place of importance in your life instead of a primary place? How would that work?

2. Read again the story of Sadan, the leprosy patient, on page 282. Do his final words seem hard to believe? Does a person have to experience an unusual form of suffering, such as leprosy, to come away with his feelings? Do people with "Western-style" difficulties, such as those Philip mentioned above, ever feel grateful for their suffering as they look back? Whose pain seems harder to handle, your own or that of someone like Sadan or Joni Eareckson, whose challenges are described on pages 281–82? What about pain is universal, regardless of its outer appearance?

Jesus' journey on earth involved much pain and suffering. Now he prepares a place for us to be with him. "You know the way to the place where I am going," he said. "I am the way and the truth and the life. No one comes to the Father except through me" (John 14:4, 6). Following Jesus means journeying as he did, through suffering and joy, toward redemption. This is the way of truthful living; this is the way to true life.

Are you at a place where you can say, like Sadan, "I am now happy that I had this disease"?

- No, I still hope and pray every day that God will change my situation and remove my pain. I can't imagine being grateful for it.
- I'm in so much pain and confusion now, I can't see beyond it. I hope someday I'll be grateful, but I'm not there yet.
- I don't think I have it in me. I've been dealing with these difficulties for some time now, and my perspective on them hasn't changed much. I think the burden will always weigh me down.

- I can say I'm glad for the *good* God has brought through my suffering. I wouldn't change that. Honestly, though, I can't quite say I'm happy about my situation overall.
- Yes, I thank God for allowing hardship in my life. I hated the hardship, but I love God in a way I never would have without walking through pain.

3. At the bottom of page 283 Philip tells of his friend's sexual drive. "Likely, he will learn fidelity the way anyone learns it, relying on discipline, community, and constant pleas of dependence," he writes. Can you share about a similar ongoing challenge you face in your life? Have you found that rather than expecting miraculous healing, you must rely on God's help through the ways Philip suggests? What has been the outcome? Or have you found that God is more inclined to act in a miraculous, decisive way than Philip suggests here?

4. *The world is good. The world is fallen. The world can be redeemed.* "Though God may not prevent the hardships of this free and dangerous world, neither did God seek personal immunity from them," writes Philip. Through Jesus, "God transformed ultimate evil into ultimate good, working through humanity's violence and hatred to accomplish our redemption" (p. 285).

   The first three sentences in this paragraph summarize the study we are now completing. As you look back on the weeks we have spent together and the ideas we've considered, how do you feel about what you've experienced?
- Yancey has some good points, but I'm not completely comfortable with his view on things. I don't feel he gives God enough opportunity to bless us and bring us joy.
- This has been a difficult study for me. I've seen God do wonderful things in life, and I would rather encourage people with hopeful stories than instruct them to accept hardship.

- I'm still digesting everything we've discussed. I think God has some work to do in me. Maybe he has some good to bring as well.
- Like Yancey, I have a long way to go. I have felt the acceptance, through this study, to be a Christian who struggles. I like the honest approach. I have more hope because I know it's all part of the journey and I'm not the only one with these struggles.

5. Take a few moments to flip back through your book or this study guide. Share with the others about which chapters or teachings were especially helpful for you. Have you gained new insights that are making a difference in the way you think or live? Were you prompted to incorporate some new practices into your spiritual life? Did God reveal something new about himself (or Jesus or the Holy Spirit)? Did you gain new understanding about the perspectives of someone close to you?

6. Review the story of Betsy on pages 286–88. Philip ends the book with these words: "The promise of Sunday seems hazy and hopelessly insubstantial. Unless, of course, it's true." What helps you, during the hazy times of your life, to keep hoping in the promise of Sunday, a time ahead when you will live in perfect goodness and joy?

Do you have any prayer needs to share with the group?

GRASPING FOR UNDERSTANDING OF MYSELF, MY GOD (10–20 MINUTES OR MORE)

Now we will spend some time considering a final personal issue. If time permits, reflect quietly on these questions for several minutes and then share together as a group.

- Is there a part of your life that needs to be redeemed by God?
- Are you holding tightly to a wound, or to a longing, circumstance, illness, disability, temptation, or fear?
- Do you need to let go before God can begin a work of redemption?
- What would it mean for you to let go?
- Do you have the courage to let go?
- How could the people in this group, or others in your life, help?
- Are you willing to accept that God's way of redeeming might look different from your expectations?
- Do you believe that God's way will be a good one?

Continue to pray about these issues in the weeks ahead.

CLINGING TO GOD DESPITE THE DISTANCE
(5–10 MINUTES)

Now we will spend some final minutes in silent prayer, offering to God our need for redemption. Pray about the bulleted questions above, wherever your current need lies. Talk with God about an area of your life in need of redemption and ask for his help in letting go, seeking help, accepting his way, or believing in his goodness. You may want to write your prayer in a journal so you can look back later and watch how God redeems.

LONGING FOR GOD IN THE WEEK AHEAD
(OPTIONAL)

You can integrate this study into your life throughout the week by using the following suggestions and readings.

- This week spend your quiet times flipping back through this study guide and reviewing the issues we studied. Focus on those themes that particularly impacted you. Review the accompanying chapters in Philip's book, Scriptures, and other readings. Ask God how he would have you continue to incorporate these themes into your life.

The following excerpt is taken from *A Long Obedience in the Same Direction* by Eugene Peterson.

There is one phrase in [Psalm 129] that good taste would prefer to delete but that honesty must deal with: "May all who hate Zion be put to shame and turned backward!" Anger seethes and pulses in the wounds. A sense of wrong has been festering. Accumulated resentment wants vindication.

However much we feel the inappropriateness of this kind of thing in a man or woman of faith, we must also admit to its authenticity. For who does not experience flashes of anger at those who make our way hard and difficult? There are times in the long obedience of Christian discipleship when we get tired and fatigue draws our tempers short. At such times to see someone flitting from one sensation to another, quitting on commitments, ducking responsibilities, bouncing from one enthusiasm to another provokes our anger—and sometimes it piques our envy. No matter that we are, on other grounds, convinced that their adulteries are an admission of boredom, that their pleasures are the shallowest of distractions from which they must return to worsening anxieties and an emptier loneliness. Still, even when we know we are doing good work which has a good future, the foolery and the enmity of these others makes a hard day harder, and anger flares.

We can't excuse the psalmist from getting angry on the grounds that he was not yet a Christian, for he had Leviticus to read: "You shall not hate your brother in your heart. . . . You shall not take vengeance or bear any grudge against the sons of your own people, but you shall love your neighbor as yourself" (Lev. 19:17–18). . . .

So we will not make excuses for the psalmist's vindictiveness. What we will do is admire its energy, for it is apathetic, sluggish neutrality that is death to perseverance, acts like a virus in the bloodstream and enervates the muscles of discipleship. The person who makes excuses for the hypocrites and rationalizes the excesses of the wicked, who loses a sense of opposition to sin, who obscures the difference between faith and denial, grace and selfishness—that is the person to be wary of. For if there is not all that much difference between the way of faith and the ways of the world, there is not much use in making any effort to stick to it. We drift on the tides of convenience. We float on fashions.

It is in the things that we care about that we are capable of expressing anger. A parent sees a child dart out into a roadway and narrowly miss being hit by a car, and angrily yells at the child, at the driver—at both. The anger may not be the most appropriate expression of concern, but it is evidence of concern. Indifference would be somehow inhuman.

And so here. The psalms are not sung by perfect pilgrims. They made their mistakes, just as we make ours. Perseverance does not mean "perfect." It means that we keep going. We do not quit when we find that we are not yet mature and that there is a long journey still before us. We get caught yelling at our wives, at our husbands, at our friends, at our employers, at our employees, at our children. Our yelling (though not all of it!) means we care about something: we care about God; we care about the ways of the kingdom; we care about morality, about justice, about righteousness. The way of faith centers and absorbs our lives and when someone makes the way difficult, throws stumbling blocks in the path of the innocent, creates difficulties for those young in faith and unpracticed in obedience, there is anger: "May all who hate Zion be put to shame and turned backward!"

For perseverance is not resignation, putting up with things the way they are, staying in the same old rut year after year after year, or being a doormat for people to wipe their feet on. Endurance is not a desperate hanging on but a traveling from strength to strength. There is nothing fatigued or humdrum in Isaiah, nothing flatfooted in Jesus, nothing jejune in Paul. Perseverance is triumphant and alive. The psalmist lived among prophets and priests who dealt with his vindictive spirit and nurtured him toward a better way of treating the wicked than calling down curses on them, learning what Charles Williams once described as the "passion of patience." We are in a similar apprenticeship. But we will not learn it by swallowing our sense of outrage on the one hand, or, on the other, excusing all wickedness as neurosis. We will do it by offering up our anger to God who trains us in creative love.[1]

NOTES

WEEK 2: DOUBT AND DIFFICULTIES

1. Ralph C. Wood, "In Defense of Disbelief," *First Things* (October 1998), 32–33.

WEEK 3: FAITH THAT WORKS

1. Brennan Manning, *Ruthless Trust* (San Francisco: HarperCollins, 2000), 4–6.

WEEK 4: DAILY FAITH

1. J. B. Phillips, *Your God Is Too Small* (New York: Touchstone, Simon & Schuster, 1997), 83–85.

WEEK 5: UNDERSTANDING GOD THE FATHER

1. http://www.ccel.org/j/julian/revelations (Christian Classics Ethereal Library).

WEEK 6: UNDERSTANDING JESUS AND THE HOLY SPIRIT

1. Philip Yancey and Brenda Quinn, *Meet the Bible: A Panorama of God's Word in 366 Daily Readings and Reflections* (Grand Rapids: Zondervan, 2000), 552–53.

WEEK 7: INNER TRANSFORMATION

1. Henri Nouwen, *Life of the Beloved* (New York: Crossroad, 1992), 59–64.

WEEK 8: PASSION AND GOD'S PRESENCE

1. Richard Foster, *Prayer: Finding the Heart's True Home* (San Francisco: HarperSanFrancisco, 1992), 124–25.

WEEK 9: MATURING IN THE FAITH

1. Brennan Manning, *Lion and Lamb: The Relentless Tenderness of Jesus* (Old Tappan, N.J.: Revell, 1986), 21.

2. Dallas Willard, *The Spirit of the Disciplines: Understanding How God Changes Lives* (San Francisco: Harper and Row, 1988), ix–xii.

WEEK 10: LIVING OUT REDEMPTION

1. Henri Nouwen, *The Living Reminder* (New York: Seabury Press, 1977), 18–22.

WEEK 11: BAD TURNED GOOD

1. Dallas Willard, quoted in John Ortberg, "The 'Shyness' of God," *Christianity Today* 45, no. 2 (February 5, 2001): 67.

2. Philip Yancey, *The Jesus I Never Knew* (Grand Rapids: Zondervan, 1995), 105–26.

WEEK 12: HOPE TO HOLD ON TO

1. Adapted from *A Long Obedience in the Same Direction* by Eugene Peterson. © 1980, 2000 by Eugene H. Peterson. Used with permission from InterVarsity Press, P.O. Box 1400, Downers Grove, IL 60515.

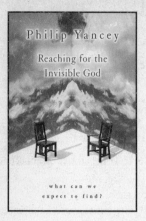

REACHING FOR THE INVISIBLE GOD

Philip Yancey

Life with God doesn't always work like we thought. High expectations slam against the reality of personal weaknesses and unwelcome surprises. And the God who we've been told longs for our company may seem remote, emotionally unavailable.

Is God playing games? What can we count on this God for? How can we know? *How can we know God?*

This relationship with a God we can't see, hear, or touch—how does it really work?

Reaching for the Invisible God offers deep, satisfying insights that affirm and dignify the questions we're sometimes afraid to ask. Award-winning author Philip Yancey explores six foundational areas: our thirst for God, faith during times when God seems unavailable, the nature of God himself, our personal relationship with God, stages along the way, and the end goal of spiritual transformation. Honest and deeply personal, here is straight talk on Christian living for the man or woman who wants more than pat answers to life's imponderables. Ultimately, Yancey shifts the focus from our questions to the One who offers himself in answer. The God who invites us to reach for him—and find.

"I love Philip Yancey's work. He is a brilliant, graceful writer."
—Anne Lamott, Author, *Traveling Mercies*

"This passionate book, unflinching in its honesty, will build your faith by helping you wrestle authentically with your doubts. Join Philip Yancey in this quest and you'll come closer still to our invisible but very real God."
—Lee Strobel, Author, *The Case for Faith*

Pick up a copy today at your favorite bookstore!

Hardcover 0-310-23531-6
Study Guide 0-310-24057-3
Audio Pages® Abridged Cassettes 0-310-23955-9
Audio Pages® Unabridged Cassettes 0-310-23477-8
E book 0-310-239-338

OTHER RESOURCES BY PHILIP YANCEY

WHAT'S SO AMAZING ABOUT GRACE?

In his most personal and provocative book ever, Yancey offers compelling, true portraits of grace's life-changing power. He searches for its presence in his own life and in the church. He asks, How can Christians contend graciously with moral issues that threaten all they hold dear? And he challenges us to become living answers to a world that desperately wants to know, *What's So Amazing About Grace?*

Hardcover 0-310-21327-4 / Study Guide 0-310-21904-3
Audio Pages® Abridged Cassettes 0-310-21578-1 / Audio Pages® Unabridged Cassettes 0-310-23228-7
Zondervan*Groupware*™ 0-310-23323-2 / Leader's Guide 0-310-23326-7
Participant's Guide 0-310-23325-9

THE JESUS I NEVER KNEW

From the manger in Bethlehem to the cross in Jerusalem, Yancey presents a complex character who generates questions as well as answers; a disturbing and exhilarating Jesus who wants to radically transform your life and stretch your faith.

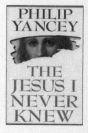

Hardcover 0-310-38570-9
Audio Pages® Abridged Cassettes 0-310-22982-0
Zondervan*Groupware*™ 0-310-22358-X
Leader's Guide 0-310-22433-2 / Participant's Guide 0-310-22433-0

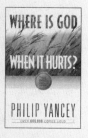

WHERE IS GOD WHEN IT HURTS?

In this Gold Medallion Award-winning book, Philip Yancey reveals a God who is neither capricious nor unconcerned. Using examples from the Bible and from his own experiences, Yancey looks at pain—physical, emotional, and spiritual—and helps us understand why we suffer.

Softcover 0-310-35411-0
Mass Market 0-310-21437-8

DISAPPOINTMENT WITH GOD

Is God unfair? Is he silent? Is he hidden? This insightful and deeply personal book points to the odd disparity between our concept of God and the realities of life. Why, if God is so hungry for relationship with us, does he seem so distant? Why, if he cares for us, do bad things happen? What can we expect from him after all? Yancey answers these questions with clarity, richness, and biblical assurance. He takes us beyond the things that make for disillusionment to a deeper faith, a certitude of God's love, and a thirst to reach not just for what God gives, but for who he is.

Softcover 0-310-51781-8
Mass Market 0-310-21436-X

We want to hear from you. Please send your comments about this book to us in care of the address below. Thank you.

ZONDERVAN™

GRAND RAPIDS, MICHIGAN 49530

www.zondervan.com